Writing Life Stories

One Piece at a Time

Marylou Bugh

Marylou Bugh
3404 Senske Rd
Standish, Michigan 48658

marylou.bugh@gmail.com

ISBN 978-0-615-96790-5

Printed in the United States of America

Dedicated to
MidMichigan Writers and
especially to Chris Lucka,
my patient editor and friend.

Table of Contents

Introduction

"I have written my life in small sketches, a little today,
a little yesterday, as I have thought of it, as I remember
all the things from childhood on through the years,
good ones and unpleasant ones, that is how they come out
and that is how we have to take them."

– Anna Mary Moses (Grandma Moses)

Why have you decided to write your life stories now? What will you discover as you write? Your family history? Your life theme? Your inner self? Will you be another Scheherazade in the Arabian Nights who prolonged her life by telling stories?

And which form will you choose? Memoir? Personal essays? Autobiography? These are the questions that may assail you as you pick up this book and take pen in hand. In these pages of introduction, you will find information that will help you answer these questions—and as you go through this book, you will find answers to much more.

First, let us consider the forms that personal stories take. Picture your life as a full jigsaw puzzle. Each piece is added in a certain way so that a design emerges from several that complete the whole. An autobiography is this 'whole picture'. We are born, grow, live our adult lives, and age. An autobiography is almost always stamped with this universal pattern of story. It usually has a chronological order—a beginning, middle and an end. Chapter one connects to chapter two and so on. It reflects on a life lived and ends with the ultimate message the writer wishes to convey. There are not many who write their autobiography and follow it with another.

Next, if you take out one piece of the puzzle, it has the consistency and color that adds to the whole, but it is a particular patterned piece. It focuses on a piece of life— "My Year as a Mime," "The Day I Left School Behind"—This is memoir. A memoir dramatizes an important part of a life, even as that particular piece is one part of the whole. It's possible that a whole life is about mimes or school, but it's more probable that mimes or school is only one part of a life filled with many other experiences. Memoirs can be as short as a few pages or as long as book length. It depends on how big that 'block' of life is for an individual. *Girl Interrupted* by Susanna Kaysen is a book-length memoir of two years in a young girl's life after she is declared insane. *Drinking the Rain* by Alix Kates Shulman is an interlude in the life of an older woman who lived alone on an island off the coast of Maine. Other memoirs are as short as six pages, as the beautifully evocative "What the End is For" by Rams Hairdo, published in *Fourth Genre's* first issue.

A personal essay has a strong relationship to a memoir, and often the relationship is so strong that trying to explain its difference is an exercise in splitting hairs. In general, a memoir often uses all the techniques of a good piece of fiction with scenes of drama and action. An essay employs less scene and plot development, but uses personal examples to explore and/or explain a universal idea, such as the 'importance of family' or 'faith that moves mountains.'. However, numerous personal essays employ story techniques as well. E.B. White's essays, especially 'Once More to the Lake' is a classic example.

Essay collections may or may not be connected by what has gone before. An essay 'First Tooth', which might talk about the milestones a child faces, could be followed by 'My Mother's Dill Pickles', an extended thought on family tradition. A book of essays has the wonderful feeling of sitting around a campfire and listening to stories connected only by the storyteller's voice. Such a collection is more open-ended than either a memoir or an autobiography, and writers from Montaigne to E.B. White to Joan Didion have spent their careers writing in this form.

A memoir or an essay collection leaves room for the writer to come back with Volume 2. As I said earlier, an autobiography is more closed. The sections of this book lend themselves more readily to the memoir or essay, but if you are in the autobiographical mode, you will still find inspiration and guidance in this book for ways to access your memories and helpful techniques to bring your story alive.

Now that we've reviewed the forms that your life story or stories can take, another question to consider before you begin is why have you decided to write your life? A clear, honest answer will inform the style and structure of the pages you generate from that white space that confronts you. If your goal is to publish, true stories are in the book world's demand and they are not just for celebrities anymore. Susanna Kaysen's memoir was a national best seller and Shulman's *Drinking the Rain* was a Los Angeles Times Book Prize finalist. Neither of these women are Hollywood stars or American presidents. They are people that coped with situations in lives similar to our own.

Theories abound in the literary world on the recent surge of interest in the memoir. It may be a collective need for roots and family stories in our fast-paced, mobile society. It may be the information age itself which wants hard 'truth' in its literary offerings. Or it may be the influence of Truman Capote's ground-breaking *In Cold Blood* that opened the way of blending factual writing with the more interesting techniques of fiction. Whatever the reason, it is a form that is marketable.

However, writing for the market involves all the skill you can muster, so your story is as compelling as a good work of fiction. (As every fiction writer knows, fiction has to read as truth.) A fine instruction in fiction that feels like truth is Carol Shields *Stone Diaries*. I thought I was reading a woman's family history until I was halfway through. Then I caught the word 'fiction' in one of those back cover comments (which I try not to read until I've read the book) and I found that I had been totally taken in. It was a wonderful book.

On the other hand, Oprah Winfrey's disappointed outrage at James Frey's infamous *A Million Little Pieces* is a lesson in keeping a story firmly in fact or fiction. Use every literary device that makes your story come alive for the reader, but stay honest to the memoir genre, or throw this book down and find one that gives you some good instruction on writing fiction.

Perhaps you are not interested in publishing at all, but want to leave your story to family and/or friends in some kind of final form. The few and scattered stories you have told are not enough to explain who you are and why you were here at all. Perhaps your memoir may not be stories at all, but more an instruction on the art of making dill pickles, or how and why you do yoga, or maybe a character sketch of

Uncle Charley who will never be known if someone doesn't describe him from his one picture in a family photo album. If your goal is to leave your story for family and friends with a series of recipes or poems or character sketches, it still needs all the skill you can muster to make your words alive and interesting. Even family will skip reading a story bogged down with sloppy sentences, breast-beating narrative or lack of structure.

As you write your stories, you may find a thread of self-discovery runs through the writing process as surely as if you had planned it. It's yet another powerful reason to write. The discovery is as individual as the person who reads these words. The self-help field is just beginning to realize the implications that the writing process has for meditation, self-healing, and knowledge. Look at the bookshelves with their many and creative offerings on ways to write journals, methods to tap the writer within, etc. In spite of all the books on the subject, there is no one way to know where the writer will connect with that core that is truly the self.

Eudora Welty expresses this phenomenon well in *One Writer's Beginnings*:

> "Writing a story is one way of discovering sequence in experience, of stumbling upon cause and effect in the happenings of a writer's own life. Connections slowly emerge. Like distant landmarks you are approaching, cause and effect begin to align themselves, draw closer together. Experiences too indefinite of outline in themselves to be recognized for themselves connect and are identified as a larger shape. And suddenly a light is thrown back, as when your train makes a curve, showing that there has been a mountain of meaning rising behind you on the way you've come, is rising there still, proven now through retrospect."

I felt a thrill of recognition when I read Welty's words, although it was not in my own memoir, but in my mother's. My mother had always promised to write her stories but as she got older, I feared they would evaporate after she was gone. A few years before her death, I interviewed her and filled eight tapes with her stories. I am now working from those tapes and see a powerful theme in her life, that 'mountain of meaning' she probably never saw herself—She had very deep faith and her beliefs supported her through the death of four daughters, an unhappy marriage, and a myriad of personal reversals. Her church's influence was not always spiritual. In her world, it was the only avenue for education and learning the niceties of life that she would never have experienced in the hard, rural environment where she grew up. I lived with my mother for years, and then I took care of her. I never saw her life theme, that thread of recognition, until I started transcribing those tapes.

From my experience with teaching the memoir, I have tried to address memoir writers of every stripe with a consistent view on quality. I looked through many books on writing life stories before I started putting this one together. In several, I found some wonderful inspirational reasons for writing memoir and a multitude of ways to access buried memories, but the writing exercises offered had few suggestions to improve the quality of those first drafts. And many books leaned heavily on the therapeutic benefits of baring one's soul by way of pen and paper with little emphasis on the unique stories a life has to offer.

I taught memoir classes to people from the ages of thirty to seventy with the goal to bring their stories to the page as powerfully as they could. We told as many stories as we wrote. Writing together made me realize that their stories could have as much impact as a Dickens or Balzac. As class confidence grew, they too realized the importance of their own life stories and they wanted those stories written in the best way possible.

Each section in this book is a 'class', an attempt to bring together the activities we did, the writing techniques we discussed and the methods of critique we used. It is meant to be a working notebook. You can use it to organize your own writing group or for your own individual use. It is meant to be a writing adventure; playful, life-affirming, fun.

Each section begins with a particular prompt to bring as many senses into your first writing as possible—the sound of music or poetry read aloud, the smell of food, fingers around a drawing pencil, or the sight of a cherished photo or a work of art. These are only a few from a multitude of possibilities. Suggestions for ways to use these prompts are included at the end of each section. The prompt will nudge other memories and you may write a story that is not about the prompt at all. Or you may focus on one or two prompts and use them to write several pieces.

There is no chronological order to the prompts. Try all the prompts at the beginning of each section or use the ones that fit. Revisit the ones that you especially like. Write from whatever occurs to you. Today it might be the first day of school, tomorrow it might be your mother's death. After you have written (and rewritten!) several pieces, you will find the form that is your favorite way of expressing yourself.

With each section, a writing technique is explained and suggestions for these are also included at the end of each section. The writing techniques are introduced in a more sequential manner and often refer to material that was covered in a previous section. I strongly suggest the first two sections that are basic to whatever you write.

Finally, good writers are good readers. They absorb the patterns and rhythms of written language and throughout my classes in writing, I always assigned readings which we analyzed together in class. I have included a bibliography of these, but I am using my own work as a reading in each section.

I have a purpose here. Besides providing a piece to analyze and critique, I want to share a working writer's process. You will see that these selections are not as good as a Mary Karr or a Jeanette Wall, but I want to share them with you, my reader, my audience. As closely as is possible, I duplicate a written piece that is brought to class, although I realize that my examples will not be as good as a live class with all its digressions and fiery debates, but each section will give you fuel for discussion if you are using the sections as a group's writing guide. We will journey together to the best story possible.

Ten Commandments
for Writing Your Memoir

I.
I am the person in command of my life and my story. I will not bring in interpretations that are not my own.

II.
I shall keep holy my work time and not use excuses to skip my writing.

III.
I will not call my writing other names like 'just fooling around' or 'my little hobby.'

IV.
I shall honor my Father and Mother by telling my stories about them as honestly as I can remember.

V.
I will not heap abuse on another, but I will not discount feelings of rage, revenge, remorse. I have felt every human emotion. I will tell how it felt in the most honest language I know how to use.

VI.
I shall not write about my sex life in any way that is uncomfortable. However, I will not step around the fact that I am a sexual human being.

VII.
I shall not steal anyone else's clichés or dramatic scenes. I will tell my story with my own language.

VIII.
I shall not lie or dodge the truth by being overly kind to myself or dishonest about others.

IX.
I shall edit and revise my words, but not the truth of my story.

X.
I shall not wish that my story is like anyone else's. I am the only one who has ever lived my life and I will love it, warts and all.

Section One

The Journal

Write fast, write everything...
Write from your feelings,
write from your body,
accept whatever comes.

— Tristine Rainier

As I said in the introduction, every writer needs this section, as well as section two. A working journal is part of a writer's tool box. Basically a journal is a collection of private writing and may include anything from grocery lists to passionate poetry. There have been whole books written on the journal and I realize that this brief section only skims the surface on the ways journals are part of a thinking person's life. If you already keep a journal, you have a valuable resource, although the following pages may give you ideas to make your journaling even better. If you don't keep a journal, the following pages will introduce you to the way various journals are kept, and you will find a system that works for you.

First, a little history, and journals have a long history. The first known journals were kept by 10th century Japanese court ladies. Much of what we know of the upper class life back then came from these women who wrote in their native Japanese because they were forbidden to use Chinese, the language of higher status at the time. Their use of their common language made their writing popular and widely read. They didn't keep day-to-day recordings but a record of subjective fantasies and fictions with long intervals between entries.

One lady wrote every seven years (Her journal must have been very short or her life very long).

In Western culture, journals did not have a very good reputation in the years of the Inquisition. Women's written words were kept by 'witches' to record spells, and journals or diaries were surrounded by mystery and magic. Their recipes of herbs and midwife practices, if discovered, were burned and often the women who wrote them were burned as well. This secretive slant on personal writing continued into this century with little diaries marketed for young girls, complete with lock and key.

However, in 17th century England, the journal took on a more accepted mode. Samuel Pepys and other 'Protestant gentlemen' used a journal to give an account of their lives to a watchful God. No witches' recipes there! The Puritans brought that journal practice over on the Mayflower, and for years children were taught to record their consciences. Emerson and Thoreau were both products of this upbringing, but their thoughts became a part of a differing philosophic view than what the Puritans had in mind.

In the years of American pioneers, women kept journaling alive and created a network of correspondence and support with written records of their lives far from the social structure that they had known. For a time, this set diaries aside as a 'woman thing' in 19th century America, a tradition that followed the country's marketing into the fifties with the pink-packaged one-year diaries that Tristine Rainier said in *The New Diary* were "as relevant to the needs of the twentieth century as lace pantaloons were to piano legs".

Then Carl Jung (1875-1961), who had been a disciple of Freud, kept an important diary filled with dreams and fantasies that he eventually believed were not unique to him, but universal in all cultural myths. His major psychological writing stemmed from the work in his journals. Marion Milner, an English psychoanalyst, in similar fashion, kept a journal for years, and came to the conclusion, through her own diaries, that human psychology was neither all Freud or all Jung, but a balance of both. Her theory, described in *A Life of One's Own*, was ahead of its time and her name is virtually unknown. Both Jung and Milner are examples of journaling as part of a thinking person's life.

After Jung and Milner, Progoff emphasized self-discovery and introduced a three-ring binder system of journal keeping, *INTENSIVE JOURNAL*, that is prescriptive and analytical and a little overwhelming. Perhaps Julia Cameron's morning pages, outlined in *The Artist's Way*, is a less intimidating method for self-discovery. She advises journal writers to write three pages as soon as they get up in the morning. Don't think. Don't edit. Just write.

As you can see, journals can include dreams, fantasies, fictions, recipes, philosophy, day-to-day activities and self discovery. A working writer's journal may be a little of all and not devoted to any one way of keeping a life in hand. At any rate, journaling should not be like Tristine Ranier's early experience (as well as my own) of 'keeping a diary' in the small restricted spaces of the fifties lock-and-key diary. Rainier said,

> "I assumed from its structure that every evening I had to fill a page with a summary of my day's activities. I came to despise that unnatural duty as I labored with pages when I had too much to say one day and apologies when I'd forgotten to write for a whole week."

My daughter, a wonderful writer, kept journals with big pages that had to lay just right, no stiff binding. She pulled her big journal out and wrote things she heard or saw in town, in her yard, or at a family reunion. She made lists, she copied quotes to remember forever and drew diagrams. She carried it everywhere and bought purses to accommodate it. She didn't know anything about the diaries of the fifties.

I would like to keep a journal like my daughter did, but I came from Tristine Rainier's generation. My official 'journal' followed the pattern that I too learned from a little dated book with only so many lines. To this day, my 'real' journal is a bunch of scattered pieces of paper on my desk that I eventually gather up and put into a folder.

What am I saying to you? Keep a journal however you like. For one thing, it keeps you writing. Often, whole entries are nothing but chatter you need to do to get to more meaningful thoughts. Put it between two covers if you can (It is much easier to find) and date the entries. Write lists, dreams, impressions, poems and character sketches. The journal belongs in the first phase of the writing process, raw material that you can use. It will be the step one of the six-step writer's process covered in the next section.

I like to make lists and my folder has all kinds of lists, some 'to do' lists (the chatter), and some that are springboards for further writing. Susan Wittig Albert in *Writing Your Life* says, "My writing notebooks are full of lists of things I want to write about, lists of words and phrases that intrigue me, memories, observations, exasperations." Note that Albert calls her journals 'notebooks'. It's a step away from recorded personal impressions locked into the "unnatural way" Tristine Rainier described in those tight, allotted pages for each entry.

The following is a brief list I made and a short piece that I wrote using the first item on the list.

What if...
    I changed my name
    I won the lottery
    I had married someone else
    I had a different job

If I changed my name, it would be Zelda. The Z has a sharp final ring to it, a sound that says I know who I am and what I want to do. The d in the second syllable holds up the name. It doesn't taper off into a sound that has to be dragged along like a limp tail, an afterthought that makes a name as weak as a sweaty handshake. It would be a good name for the second half of my life, a signifier that I am sharper and stronger.

I don't know any Zeldas. It would be a name without memory traces—no family legends to live down or live up to, no characteristics to banish. Of course there was F. Scott Fitzgerald's notorious wife, but she seems far away from my own history.

If a new name is far away from my own history, I will reinvent myself. I will wear outrageous clothes and write books that shock and challenge. I will go to book signings with a purple-plumed pen and scrawl Zelda in a large bold script for strangers who will look at me and wonder at how I came to be the person I am.

Since I write fiction, I may use some of this in one of my stories. Or I may never use it at all. But if I hadn't put it in my journal, I wouldn't have captured the idea. Odd thoughts flit into our minds, characters strike us, a line to remember that we heard or read that we want. That's why it's important to keep a journal. It won't stay otherwise. Show up every day, pen in hand. If you keep the door open, you never know what might come in.

Exercises

- ∞ Go shopping. Find a journal that's the right size, lays flat and has the right area for writing or sketching that is comfortable for you. Don't settle for anything less.

- ∞ Date every entry.

- ∞ Use your journal on a regular basis. Keep it handy to jot down a fleeting impression. If the idea of keeping a journal is new and you can't think of a thing to write, write about the pencil laying on your desk or the moth flying around your lamp.

- ∞ Find a word, any word, in a book, a magazine, or a dictionary. Use the word in your first sentence and then keep writing (this is an exercise similar to webbing explained in section two). Don't get trapped into defining the word.

- ∞ Make a list of everything you have to do tomorrow and then write why you won't do them. I know—you'll do them anyway— but pretend.

- ∞ Draw a checkerboard with you, a figure in the middle (you can use a real photo if you want). On the squares closest to you, write or draw or paste pictures of the things that are the most important. Fill in the spaces further out with the parts of your life that are more distant. Circles work too.

- ∞ Sketch, diagram, make lists, invent recipes, copy quotes, or write hate letters or love letters that you'll never send.

∞ Try this:

Line one: How I see myself as a color.
Write four words or phrases that explain your choice
Example: yellow > warm, mellow, cheerful, country.

Line two: How you see yourself as an animal.
Again, use four words or phrases to explain your choice
Example: Hound dog > friendly, happy, eager to satisfy, not fussy.

Line three: How I feel about sex in four words or phrases.
Use an earth symbol here.
Example: ocean > varied moods, powerful, crashing and receding, all encompassing).

Line four: How you feel about death.
Again, using the same format.

Further Suggestions for Finding Your Stories

Making lists is an active memory process. Somewhere in these lists will be the car or the pet or the game that yields a bigger story.

∞ List people who made the biggest impact on your life. Find three words to describe them.

∞ List friends of your parents, your neighbors, relatives, class mates. Some may spark memories of characters to add to your stories. List clubs, religious affiliations, community functions, etc. These may add settings. List family pets, cars, favorite clothes, toys you cherished, etc. These may trail into childhood stories you thought you had forgotten.

∞ List five rules of your family. Who made them? How were they enforced? How easy or how hard was it to change them?

- Family communication: Do you have any family sayings? What was the noise level of your home? Body language? Slang terms used? Voice tones? (All of this adds vivid detail to your scenes.)

- Describe a family mealtime. Favorite foods? Traditions at a holiday meal? Who sits where at the table?

- Describe "a day in the life of_____ (Deviation from the normal adds good story tension, such as "John did not come home at his usual time.)

- Family legends: Most families have stories repeated over and over at family get-togethers until they have the semblance of a legend. (We even have stories of the great Rebel, our favorite family dog.) Write a brief narrative of a family story. Enlarge it with scenes and details.

- Construct a family totem, each family member represented with an animal face. Or make a logo or icon that represents each one. Write a reflection on your choices.

Section Two

The Writing Process

*A work of art is not a matter of thinking beautiful thoughts or
experiencing tender emotions (though those are its raw materials)
but of intelligence, skill, taste, proportion, knowledge, discipline
and industry; especially discipline.*

– Evelyn Waugh

No one likes to think that they are predictable, especially artists.
But writing is an art comparable to drawing, painting or sculpture. In each, there is a basic set of materials, techniques applied to a chosen medium, and a process that turns the medium and the material into a finished piece. The process is the same whether you are Hemingway or Picasso; the difference is in the time that artists spend with each part of the process. Those who have an intimate knowledge of their medium may fold two steps into such tight succession, it may seem they skip steps altogether. Or they spend little time on one that is their strength and a lot of time with another. But a good piece of art does not come full and wonderful out of nowhere.

Before artists begin work, they need to know their materials and have those tools on hand. That's basic. Compared to visual artists who work with oils or clay, writers' tools are simple; besides a working journal, a writer uses paper and pen, a dictionary, a thesaurus, and a basic grammar book such as *Strunk and White.*

A computer and scanner are the most recent tools in a writer's work space that may take time to know, although some writers, especially poets, don't and won't have either and write longhand and even use a

9

typewriter for their final drafts. The physical act of writing puts some writers' minds into a creative side that keyboarding doesn't replicate.

Endless writers' discussions can revolve on the right pen, the right paper, the right place to write. Faulkner said, "The tools I need are paper, tobacco, food, and a little whiskey." Steinbeck said, "Pencils must be round. A hexagonal pencil cuts my fingers after a long day." And Isaac Bashevis Singer advised that "The wastepaper basket is the writer's best friend." (Evidently, Singer knew the writing process intimately).

Writers' tools and how they are used are as individual as the particular pen in hand or the preferred keyboard, but the way the writer molds and remolds that first draft, from those first words that come to the paper or computer screen, are all part of a predictable writing process. Pat Conroy in *My Reading Life* says, "Good writing is one of the forms that hard labor takes. It is taking the nothingness of air and turning it into a pleasure palace built on a foundation of words." The first draft has a few gold nuggets and a lot of silt. The art of good writing comes in sifting out the silt and shaping the gold, the way writers get words down on paper and then take that raw material and polish it. I will discuss sifting the silt and shaping the gold, even as I recognize that each writer will adapt my recipe to his/her own style.

The Writing Process

1. Prewrite. This is the kick-start to what you have to say. It is an active mind process and at first may not necessarily have a thing to do with pen and paper. In the pre-write phase, words occur while a writer does dishes, vacuums, welds, walks, stares at the moon, or awakens from a dream. Then thoughts are recorded into a working journal, a mind map, whether those fleeting thoughts are expressed as a list, a phrase, a sketch or a diagram. The writing prompts in the following sections are nudges to encourage the prewrite phase.

2. First draft. This is the first writing after a phrase, a dream, an idea that gets you started. Write without thinking about mechan-

ics or structure. Get it down on paper. Don't stop writing for at least fifteen minutes.

After that first burst of writing, try looping. Read over what you have written and underline a key phrase or two. Start a new free write with that phrase and write again for fifteen minutes. Again, read over your words and find a key phrase. Continue until you have exhausted your topic.

This is the first draft. It will have a lot of silt, but it will have some gold too. William Least Heat-Moon said that he destroys all his first drafts so no one will ever see how bad his first writing is. This first-draft writing does not look pretty but it will produce the words, phrases, sentences or paragraphs that you will use in your final work. Beautiful prose in *Blue Highways* came from William Least Half-Moon's bad writing.

3. Revise or rewrite. After the first burst of writing, read what you have written. You will begin to see the 'main idea' that our English teachers always pointed out back in those formal outline days. Don't be surprised if the main idea is not what you thought it would be when you wrote that first sentence. Often, you will find that a sentence or paragraph buried in the middle of your work is the one that names your major idea. Cut and paste it at the beginning. See how you can loop that idea around so that it echoes at the end of your piece.

This is where you learn to trust the real story that is inside somewhere and comes out in that first draft, a story that you didn't expect. This is the magic of writing that never ceases to amaze me, and one of the reasons I write. It's the 'voice' of the writer that is you. It is hard to describe, but first writing often captures that individual way you express yourself.

But now comes the other side, the steely-eyed editor with the red pen, the part of you that revises: a.) Delete sentences or sections that do not relate to the major idea. b.) Add details to enrich or explain your major idea. c.) Rearrange details that belong elsewhere in the story. d.) After you move sentences and paragraphs to your satisfaction, underline every passive verb with a red marker. Underline every prepositional phrase with a

11

blue marker, every adverb with a green one, every adjective with a purple one (Refer to 'Grammar Gremlins' at the end of this section). If you have too many reds (passive verbs such as 'am', 'is', 'are', 'was' and 'were') replace with active verbs. Often you will have to redo a sentence. If you have too many blues, minimize prepositional phrases that can bog down your sentences. Likewise, look at those green adverbs, which should be used with the utmost discretion

4. When you have revised the piece to the best of your ability, read it to other listeners/ readers for critique. This audience is your 'first readers'. You might bring a glaze to their eyes, or you might hear their laughs or sighs or sense their interest. If you left something out, they will tell you they were confused. If you put in too much, they will tell you where they were bored. Take detailed notes on their comments.

    I'm lucky to have a group, MidMichigan Writers, people who come from three counties twice a month to read their work to each other. At the end of this section, I've included the workshop critique we use. It's easy for a moderator to work with and yet it has never failed to provoke great discussions and keep listeners/readers on track.

    If you don't have a group, see if you can start one. And if you don't have listeners, read your work aloud into a tape recorder. It's the next best thing to a live audience. As you listen back, don't look at your written pages. Just listen with pad and pen in hand as if the voice is a person you never heard before. Every time you hear a word or a sentence that 'clunks' or is unclear or out of place, make a note. Go back and fix it as soon as you've finished listening. If you are a writer alone, adapt the steps of reading aloud the best you can to the critique guidelines as if your work was not yours, but the work of someone else.

    A word of caution with finding listeners. Family or close friends are not the best choices for critique. Either they know your stories too well or they will not want to seem 'critical'.

5. Revise again after you've garnered all the input you can find. This is the hardest part. It's taking the gold that you've worked

with, and worked with again, and now you have to put the final form to it. Maybe a sentence or a paragraph added, maybe getting rid of the paragraph you loved. It's a hard step and it drives you beyond what you think you can do. Sometimes you can get there and make it work, and sometimes you have given it all you've got and you don't have the final insight to make it shine like you want. This *is* the hardest part.

6. Put your piece into a final draft. You might have to do steps 3-5 more than once on a longer piece, section by section. Make each the best you can produce. Love it. If you keep writing, your next story will be better.

I've listened to or read writers' drafts from third grade children to grandmothers of seventy and watched them go through the writing process, and saw the pride in their eyes after they have wrestled with the whole writing process and finally said what they really wanted to say. The first step in writing is dispelling the idea that the first writing comes out perfect. Even Hemingway couldn't do it. He stood at a little podium and wrote one page at a time, rereading every word he wrote. In a whole morning, he usually produced two or three pages. Now that you've looked at the steps in the writing process, you may have already reached the conclusion that Hemingway went through the whole process with each page. No, he didn't have a listener, but I would bet that he vocalized every sentence he wrote. "It's not the writing that's difficult," he once said. "It's the rewriting."

No one writes once! As you write and edit, problem areas will come up again and again. Some writers forget to add details that enhance their stark prose. Other writers embellish their words with too many. No artist ever got it right the first time. The writing process works. But don't cheat. Step two was the raw silt with the nuggets of gold. Step three is the emerging outline. Step four and five are the push to a finished piece.

After you have done your best, put your piece away and take it out three weeks later—or three months—or six months. Read it aloud again. You will be amazed at the faults you find in what you thought was immaculate prose. A few years ago I got a new computer and my other computer was so obsolete I couldn't put my files into the new one at all. I ended up keyboarding all my 'finished' work into the new system. I don't have to tell you the moral of my sad technological tale—I reworked almost every one of the stories I thought were finished.

When you look at the following critique guidelines for the first time, you may be confused at the terms used. You may also notice that each guideline emphasizes different aspects of a story, which is why I've offered two. As you work through the following sections in this book, the terms will become clear, and one of these guidelines will become your favorite—or you may devise your own, using elements of both. At any rate, these pages are meant to be revisited over and over again. When I hear great writers say that they revise six times, twenty-six times, I know that a critique guideline is something we need to have in hand after we write.

One caution in using these guidelines: They are meant for a fully developed story and I realize that you may not be using every element of a fully developed story. You may write an extended caption for a photo or a brief memory of a family recipe. However, there are some elements that hold true no matter what the form. For instance, if you litter your prose or poetry with too many passive verbs or overused adjectives, you are using sentence patterns that are sapping the vitality and strength from your writing.

MidMichigan Writers Group Critique Guidelines

The writer is encouraged to offer the piece to members by way of email attachment or with extra copies at the meeting, although some members prefer to listen without written copy. Although the writer specifies beforehand the audience the work is intended for (children's story, memoir for family, etc.), after a member reads a piece, s/he is not allowed to talk while the critique is going on, This is to ensure that the writer is getting valid feedback. In the real world, the writer won't be sitting by the reader or editor's side to explain what the story means. The critique is coming from first readers reacting to the words that are on the page. After discussion is over, the writer can comment on the feedback.

Moderator addresses the group:

- ☙ What did you like about this piece? Remember: We build on our strengths. If the writer hears what *works*, then s/he can do more of it. Where in the story did you get interested? Was it at the first sentence, the first paragraph or somewhere in the middle? Stories have to have a 'hook' that captures interest immediately (The author might need to move a section to the beginning of your story).

- ☙ How would you describe the narrative voice? A story teller? A suave commentator? An incredulous bystander? Does the narrative voice work for the story that is being told?

- ☙ Every story has to have a reason for the telling. What is the reason for telling this story? Is it threaded throughout the story so that it is effective?

- ☙ If the piece has scenes, what are the scenes *doing* in the story? If they are not building tension towards the final climax, how could they be better? (More/better dialogue, details?) Does a scene need to be deleted to strengthen the story's focus?

- ☙ Were you confused about any part of the story? It might be a transition problem (The author may have to add a phrase or sentence to signal time or place change).

- ☙ Are there too many details? Not enough? Details that do not add to the story are dead wood. Tell the writer which details do or do not work.

- ☙ How could the language be improved? Look at grammar gremlins here, especially passive verbs.

Grammar Gremlins

Sentence run-ons: Two sentences, usually short, that the writer did not separate with punctuation. Example: I run out of the room I do not have my shoes on.

Present tense vs. past tense: Verbs determine the past or present tense of a sentence. Example: I run out of the room. I do not have my shoes on. These sentences are in present tense, action happening now (run, do). Compare with past tense: I ran out of the room. I did not have my shoes on. The verbs (ran, did) put the action in the past. Most storytelling has been traditionally in the past tense; whichever tense you choose, keep it consistent. Mixing tenses does not work.

Passive voice vs. active voice: Again, the verb decides. Example: Aunt Millie was a busy woman. Is, are, was, were, and am, are verbs of 'being' and are passive. Good writing avoids the passive as much as possible. Find every one you have on a page and highlight it. If there are more than two or three passive verbs per page, you are probably writing in a passive voice. The active voice uses 'doing' verbs. Example: Aunt Millie bustled around the kitchen. 'Bustled' is an active verb that not only denotes action, but describes the action as that of a busy woman.

Prepositional phrases: Prepositions are words such as under, over, with, by, in, before, beside and there are many more. Prepositional phrases pop up in our sentences all over the place and often we need them. However, they can rob a sentence of its strength and two or more prepositional phrases strung together slow a sentence down and often can be deleted if the right verb is used. (Example: She walked away with the table. 'She carried the table away' is more active. Highlight prepositional phrases in your work. Are you using more than a few on each page? Can you restructure your sentences?

Adverbs: Adverbs describe an adjective or a verb and are usually unnecessary if a stronger verb is used. "She timidly walked away" could be "She crept away". (There are at least twenty verb choices for the act of walking: stride, slink, creep, amble, saunter, etc.) A good verb makes your prose twice as strong.

Self Critique for Complete Story*

1. First sentence or first paragraph: How is it 'instructing' the reader to read the rest of the story?

2. "Why now" aspect. Every story has an unstable situation and precipitating event. Identify the precipitating event, the 'why now' of the story.

3. What is the time covered in the actual plot? Time factors: flashback, interior monologue. Is the story moving forward or do these time factors slow the story?

4. Map out plot by boxing each scene. Where is the climactic scene? Do all scenes point to the climactic scene? Where is the perception shift?

5. What is the dissonance in each scene? Find 'but' constructions.

6. What is this story *about*? How do the scenes move the story toward that theme?

7. Construct a paradigm for the story to relate cause and effect. Because_____ happened, then _____ happened. Do cause and effect fit with the plot and the character?

8. Do images reoccur? Do they relate to the plot?

9. Is the narration of the story ironic, sentimental, or judgmental? The narrative has to keep that voice throughout.

10. Line by line editing: Throw out passive verbs, prepositional phrases, and clichés. Watch for 'pet' words that are repeated, sentence length, and the end word of a sentence.

    Answer each question with a written response.

*I realize that this self-critique introduces many unfamiliar terms, but later on, you may find it valuable as you work through your writing process. I've found that answering each item with a written response effectively targets where a story needs fixing. The following explanation of terms might be easier than flipping through a glossary at the end of the book.

An unstable situation and a precipitating event are the reasons you have chosen to write about this photo or that recipe, or why you have chosen to write a complete story. Stories come from the events that rock a life—victories, accidents, arguments, important rituals such as weddings, births, funerals. That's the precipitating event. The unstable situation comes from you or another character's reactions to the event. A cousin's victory at becoming mayor makes you bitter. S/he has always been a thorn in your side. The first birth of your grandchild fills you with fear. Your first child's birth was a matter of life and death. The character sketch you have chosen to write about Uncle Charlie brings up memories of his abusive teasing. You chose to record the memories that had a powerful effect on you because of your unstable situation and an event that brought it to light.

The perception shift is the other reason you are telling a particular story. If you are at the wedding of your child and you cry, you cry for a reason—You finally know, really know, your child is now an adult, or your tears are a realization of your own failed marriage, or you are joyful to tears that your child will someday have the same wonderful relationship you have—whatever brings you to tears is a 'perception shift'. Something in the bedrock of your life has just experienced an earth tremor. From the unstable situation and the precipitating event, you have learned something you didn't know before. The climactic scene is where that perception shift happens.

Dissonance or the 'but' construction gets a story going and keeps it going. I thought I was happy BUT—A good story, a good scene in a story, always has that 'but'. It's the dissonance that builds tension. If you are happy, there's no story. It's a stable situation. If you are not happy, the reader wants to know why and what you did to try and fix it.

Time in a story is important and often a story shifts from what is happening now (the forward motion of plot) to a memory of what has happened before the 'now'. That's flashback, and it can be a whole scene. You are at your son's wedding and you remember in detail your own wedding with all the details of where it happened, the words spoken, the people who were there. It could be a whole scene. Or it could be an interior monologue as you are thinking that your son's wedding has more flowers and more relatives than your own had. Either way, the story has shifted from the 'now' to the past, and the reader has to have a clear signal that a time shift has happened.

Narration is the way a writer tells the story, and it influences description, dialogue and plot. If you are a writer with a sense of humor, you might describe the minister at your son's wedding as a man who looked as if he had forgotten to check the snow of dandruff on his dark suit. If you are writing as a critical parent, you would describe him as a slovenly man who should be replaced by someone up to your standards.

Getting Ready

1. Find a handy place for those colored pens that you will use in your revisions as well as a spot in your living space that is your writing corner. It may be the corner of your dining room table or the front seat of your car.

2. Get a tape recorder that is almost as comfortable as your journal. It doesn't need to be high quality, but it does need to be the right size to use in your work space.

3. Try prewriting as outlined in *Writing the Natural Way* by Gabrielle Lusser Rico. She details a 'web' that has been adopted and used by hundreds of writers. There is even a book out for visual artists using the same system. Rico talks of our random thoughts in the same way that I talk about journal entries. Her method works much of the time. We all web in our heads. Often this graphic representation helps:

    First, take a word such as 'mother', 'family', 'picnic', 'tree', whatever. Write it in the middle of a page and draw a circle around it. Then, as quickly as possible, draw lines out from the original circle. Write words or phrases that connect with that original word. Don't think, just do. Keep drawing circles, writing words, and drawing lines that connect between the words until nothing else comes to mind.

19

Then write. As random as your writing might seem, your mind uses the words and concepts that you have 'webbed' or 'clustered' (the construction does look like a web).

4. Use the critique guidelines to shape what you have written in exercise three.

5. Write your own grammar gremlin examples, both the incorrect and/or sloppy versions and the better versions. This exercise will alert you to the particular gremlins that creep into your writing.

Now that the tools are assembled, let's go into your stories that deserve the best expression you can give to them. *In the following sections, a discussion of a particular prompt will be followed by a selected writing technique. Even if you do not use the prompt, you will find the writing technique valuable in all your writing.*

Section Three

Everyday Objects

There is one trait that marks the writer.
He is always watching. It's a kind of trick
of mind and he is born with it.

– Morley Callaghan

Your home reflects who you are and the progress of your life as surely as a written history. Archeologists can unearth a shard of pottery or a whittled spoon and construct a whole life story 2,000 years ago. If your abode was unearthed in 2,000 years, what would your story be? How and why did you choose the furniture you have? Is your space decorated with particular objects like vases, posters or figurines? Or do you have a vase here, a teddy bear there, disparate objects from particular times in your life? If you could only leave one artifact to express who you are, what would it be?

The choice of furniture is powerful. For instance, family laughter is shared, decisions are made and tears are shed around a kitchen table. I have a trestle table, no leaves, and six chairs. The table doesn't fold or expand or spin. It sits on two solid trusses and stretches from one side of my kitchen to the other. I never saw a table so definite in its structure. A few years ago I thought I wanted a round oak table like the ones I saw in all the furniture ads. My sons hauled the trestle table out and replaced it with an oak table. And I didn't like it. My sons dragged the oak table out and replaced it with the trestle table.

I was as appalled as they were at my strange vacillation. After some thought, I saw that my trestle table had a corner where I piled my mail, a spot where I watched the field across the road and the corner that I used when I talked on the telephone. The round table did not give me any corners. It was too democratic. I have my suspicions about my character from the things that decorate my space and when you analyze your surroundings, the choices come right out of who you are.

Furniture is often more than an expression of your own comfort zone. Furniture that occupies your memories can also express powerful characterization; Grandpa's worn blue recliner, his chunky end table piled with his newspapers and magazines, sister's vanity with the big glass mirror, the book case your son had in college. Furniture that may look bland to others can nudge memoir writers into a personal memory zone that yields a rich family story.

However, some prefer a crisp environment that holds few reminders of past times. Others fill their space with memorabilia. Perhaps the objects are gifts from loved ones or souvenirs connected with trips or friends. Perhaps the mementos are part of a family history. My mother grew house plants. She borrowed slips from neighbors, she filled the kitchen window with potted plants and found plant stands wherever she could. And now to me, a kitchen is not a kitchen if house plants don't fill the windows. Mom also loved books and magazines and photos, and I won't go into how many bookshelves and boxes of photos I have. Sometimes our history can run over us!

Arrangement is also an interesting indicator of a person. Do you display objects in an intentional way, or do they appear and disappear in your living space with your spring cleaning?

Some display objects to draw immediate attention. Others crowd disparate mementos wherever space is available. Still others line shelves in special cabinets with valuable collectibles made by the same artist or distributed by the same company, while others leave expensive objects in precarious spots. One of my friends kept an expensive vase within reach of her young grandchild. "Children need to be around beautiful things too," she said. That said a lot about her character.

We learn to take our surroundings for granted and hardly see them in their familiarity. Really look at your shelves, your walls, your furnishings. When you focus on why you possess that wall hanging or tiny statue, the artifact trails your memory into a whole life scene, a story that you walk past a dozen times a day. The wall hanging came from a shopping excursion with a friend you no longer have, a tiny statue an item you bartered away from a Greek shop owner on an unforgettable trip. The objects become 'boss images' in a story about your friend or the tiny shop you found in Greece (I talk about 'boss image' in the next pages).

The objects around you become not only memory prompts but important details in life stories. Half of the popularity of TV shows such as "American Pickers" and "Pawn Stars" arise from the stories related to the objects considered, and PBS's "History Detectives" that starts with a found object always sheds light on a character or time in history we never read about in high school. We love stories about why a certain object or objects are kept or coveted by others. If you write, "Thirty hats hang on my bedroom wall, and I wear one every time I leave the house", the reader already has an impression of character and a curiosity about those hats.

You will find that the environment you have created for yourself and your family also echoes in the way you express yourself, your writing style. You may adorn your sentences with many details, or you may use details sparingly. Both styles of writing have been effectively used by literary giants. William Faulkner could carry on a sentence with eccentric details that lasted for a whole paragraph. Ernest Hemingway wrote without much description at all. Every writer comes from their own space, and every reader wants to be in that space, whether it's seeing a rough front porch or a Paris street . I'm not sure what Hemingways's or Faulkner's personal space looked like, but I can bet that each had to either add or subtract from their first drafts.

The Importance of Details

Details are much more than idle flourishes. They establish setting and characterization and give your story a freshness and originality. They come from your observations, that "trait that marks the writer… always watching", as Morley Callaghan said. If you are not "born with it', you can still learn to slow down and really look at the world around you.

Details are concrete images that appeal to the senses. The more senses brought into a written piece, the more likely the reader becomes a part of the experience. We tend to call up images that appeal to our own dominant senses. A writer sensitive to sight or hearing, as a majority of the population is, will invoke images that rely on those senses to the exclusion of the others. A green shirt, of course, goes to the sense of sight. How does that shirt feel or smell? Using another sense sharpens a detail in a new fresh way and reflects a different perspective about an object that you thought you had memorized.

The economy of right details can bring a whole picture to mind. As Janet Burroway says,

> "A number of ideas not stated reverberates off the sense images so that we are aware of a number of generalizations the author might have made, but does not need to make. We will make them ourselves."

The writer's image may differ from the reader's, but if details are well-chosen and concrete, the reader will fashion a clear and specific image that is close to his/her own experience and be satisfied that the story did its job. The writer's image of Dad's green shirt might be a different shade than the reader's, but with the right details, the reader will also know that the green shirt represents a bigger importance such as the youthfulness of Dad or his abysmal clothes sense.

Details spice writing but, as any good cook knows, spices have to be handled with care. If you sprinkle every noun with a plethora of details, the effect numbs the reader with excess. I recall a friend who said of a book that every line included a detail, a metaphor, a simile, and trying to read it was like swimming in molasses. She never finished the book.

Details not only lose their strength if they are excessive, they can also warp the story's focus if they are unrelated. A vivid description of bird song followed by an equally vivid detail of the dishes in Mother's china cabinet confuses what is important. If Dad's green shirt is mentioned once and other details follow that are not related to color or articles of clothing, a powerful statement about Dad's character is lost, and may leave the reader 'swimming in molasses'. Once you recognize in your first draft the main image (part three of the writing process), details that enhance that image follow this 'boss' image (or image patterning in more conventional terms). Predominant details come right out of your first draft. The wall hanging from a shopping excursion with a friend, the small statue that you bartered away from a Greek shop owner represent and resonate the whole meaning of the story.

An adjective is the simplest detail—blue sky, green grass—you are already bored. Adjectives, used often and without thought, bog down a sentence. Use them sparingly and out of context. Unlinking a word from its usual usage makes new connections. For instance, a 'ramshackle house' is predictable—ramshackle is always used to describe a building. But 'ramshackle love', ramshackle, used out of its usual context, gives the reader a special image of that relationship. If you follow that new connection with words such as 'shabby', 'dilapidated' or 'decrepit', you are creating a boss image by controlling the details that invoke the impression you want to make.

Comparisons ("as small as an ant's freckle") or contrasts ("not the white of a lily, but the white of dead skin") come from the 'always watching' writer's first draft. Details can be fashioned into effective comparisons or contrasts if they fit the context of a particular story. Beware of hackneyed clichés (green as grass) that will take away from your story instead of adding the color that you intend. In this age of media overload, clichés creep into our speech at a faster pace than ever. The first time I heard "He's not the sharpest tool in the shed', I liked it. I repeated it and repeated it again. So did everybody else. It's not fresh and unusual anymore. To rescue those 'nowisms', you could invent 'newisms': "He's a pussy willow in a forest of oaks" etc.

In your first draft, underline each noun and decide if the word itself could be changed: house to home, vehicle to truck. Specific nouns work as details in themselves. Can you invest any with an unusual adjective that enhances the story's image? Look at each detail you've already written. Find the 'boss image'. Keep the details that fit that image. Throw away those that do not add to an 'idea that you want to reverberate'. Sometimes you have to throw away the lines you love. (I don't throw them away. I put them in my journal.) To go back to Faulkner/ Hemingway, your strength in writing can be a weakness. If you write good details, you may write too many. If you write too sparingly, you will have to add.

Both of these pieces came from objects that I've had on my dresser for years and it was only now, using the object reference as a prompt that I really looked at them. I wrote "First Love" by focusing on a jewelry box, the last gift I received from my husband before we divorced. "You, Sister" came from my grandmother's dresser set that my brother-in-law gave me after my sister died.

First Love

You, my love—I first saw you at Eastman's Gravel Pit on a hot July afternoon when the air was full of cicada song and the water slid over our swimming bodies, a cool gift. I had known you with those corduroy pants in grade school, which nobody else wore. You never played with the rest of the neighborhood kids. I didn't know how you spent your early years while I chased across hay fields and bayed at the moon on Donelly's bayou, wearing ice skates that didn't fit and weren't sharp. And then, like a stranger at our swimming hole, you were there that summer. And we weren't little kids anymore.

That fall you took me duck hunting, the mist rising cold around us and the sun a ghostly yellow orb—and you were so intense and serious, I thought you knew something that I didn't know. After we conceived a child and married, the things we both learned were sad and serious. We were fastened to each other with our young intensity, living in a trailer with no running water and a baby as wonderful as if he had been fashioned from October mists. But life wasn't skating on the bayou and howling at the moon anymore.

And how was it we grew up through those years of blueberries and gardens with cucumbers and fried green tomatoes? And how was it we finally had our own house whose windows we patched with plastic against the winter cold? How was it we grew four children through those years of love and hate and passion? No time for the patter of little feet—mud tracked in during spring fishing, snow dragged in on snowmobile boots that left black marks on the kitchen floor, sand in the summer that fell from damp bathing suits. How was it our children grew up in spite of us and blew away like milkweed seeds, fine and free on the autumn air?

We harvested a huge garden that last year and got ready for another winter. But we were like empty husks after the seeds have flown, our passion crumpled and brown. We ended our days together, ended our life together—you intense and serious and I once more howling at the moon.

You, Sister

You are the sister that came four years before me. You got a lipstick first, your period first, your class ring first and a boyfriend for the prom that I never did get. I wore the dresses that you had outgrown and tried to catch up.

You ignored me when Greg Knoll picked you up for the prom and didn't introduce me even though I hung by the kitchen door waiting. Waiting. After you left in that wonderful white dress that spread out in a whisper of taffeta and net, I went out by the barnyard and hung over the fence in the twilight. I can't remember what I thought, but I hung over that fence wanting something I wasn't ready for or able to do like you were.

When I borrowed your lipstick—Pink Rapture—No, I didn't steal it—I just wanted to try it on—I turned it way out of the tube so that it looked like the ones in the drugstore ads. It broke off and stained the dresser scarf and you got so mad you hit me and I screamed. Mom made me sit by the refrigerator for an hour.

I don't know if you were mad because I ruined your lipstick or mad because I ruined the dresser scarf. You had to share a room with me and I left my Elvis Presley records on the floor and clothes wherever I stepped out of them. You knew how rooms were supposed to look. When we grew up and had homes of our own, you kept yours like a doll house. When we had children, you knew how to burp babies and keep diapers from smelling. Your babies looked like kids that never spit up on your shoulder, the kind of kids in baby food commercials. My babies looked good for at least a half hour after their bath. My house never looked like a doll house.

You were always Mom's older daughter, the one who did all those things with her that I never knew how to do. You took her shopping, you bought her things she didn't think she needed and loved after she had them. Because of you, she had a microwave and an electric coffee pot, and a recliner that she always regarded as a little decadent, but relished nonetheless.

And when you were dying with cancer and they said you couldn't talk anymore, you did. You talked to me. You told me to take care of Mom.

And that's how I got the place I had always tried to get. And like one of your outgrown dresses, it doesn't fit me well.

These are not whole stories, but rather intense pieces that were pulled from a place inside myself that I really didn't know was there. Notice that neither piece referred to the object that set these memories into motion. After the first draft of "First Love", an abundant use of outdoor details emerged that fit my life with my ex-husband. We both came from a country background and lived outdoors—fishing, hunting, gardening, and snowmobiling. And so, in the rewrite, 'outdoors' became the boss image.

If I had ended, "The wind was blowing, a typhoon, a cacophony of the gods, crying at my indecision in this marriage that I had entered without weighing the fates that were even now at my door," I would have to delete it. For one thing, a typhoon comes from a culture not even remotely connected to Michigan. Then, in the same sentence, I jump cultures again with 'a cacophony of the gods' and 'fates at my door'. To go back to step two in the writing process, these kinds of sentences fill our first drafts. Maybe I had read a Greek tragedy the night before I started writing or maybe I had seen something on TV about typhoons—these influences touch our first drafts all the time. But when you are the steely-eyed editor, you throw out lines that don't reverberate in the piece as a whole.

Likewise, the details in "You Sister" do not relate to the original prompt (as I mentioned in section two, often the main ides of the first draft is not what you thought it would be), but are loaded with young female details—lipstick, a prom dress, a doll house, details that I was especially sensitive to in those days of growing up in the shadow of a sister who handled a girl's life with an ease I struggled to emulate.

I don't need to tell the reader that I was filled with envy by my sister's savvy just as I didn't need to tell the reader that my marriage was filled with some great outdoor times. The ruined lipstick and scattered Elvis Presley records say 'messy young sister' just as doll house and kids from baby food commercials say 'neat and organized mother'. To repeat Janet Burroway, the details make the reader "aware of a number of generalizations the author might have made, but does not need to make". The reader not only experiences the story from sensory details, they also read a bigger meaning from the writer's conscious choice of words.

Finally, I want to point out an element in both pieces not related to detail at all. Both were written addressing the other as 'you', an unusual point of view (more on point of view later).

Prompt (Object) Exercises

- List the artifacts in your home with a brief description of each. This could be the organizing rule behind a memoir.

- Focus on one object and write the story of where it came from. Use details!

- Gather three or four random objects and use all the objects in a rapid free write. I might add here that objects in your world that can also prompt memories might be as mundane as certain cherished clothes in your bedroom or tools in your kitchen.

꘎ Dig out the thing you have stowed on the back shelf of a closet or remember an item from your last rummage sale. Write why the items have been put away or discarded.

꘎ Pretend you are writing for an auctioneer's brochure. Give your loved objects or furniture the description that will sell them.

꘎ If a thief broke in and took one object, what would hurt you the most? Why? Which would hurt you the least? Why?

꘎ Pretend one item from your home occupies a shelf in a museum 400 years into the future. Write a museum guide's lecture to visitors about life in your day.

Detail Exercises

꘎ Make a list of nouns. Write a phrase of comparison or contrast after each that describes it in an original way. For instance, if you list the word 'dress', don't just describe it as "blue as the sky". Compare it to something concrete in your life: 'gray as Mrs. Milmot's sheets'.

꘎ Look at your last piece of writing. Find every flat reference, such as 'their house' or 'my kitchen' and add one specific detail such as 'their house with the front porch hanging on like a forlorn relative'. Now go back and see which details are connected to a 'boss image'.

꘎ Fold a sheet of paper in half lengthwise. On the left hand side of the paper, list ten nouns. Turn the folded sheet over. On the right hand side list ten verbs that apply to a profession: For instance, a carpenter's verbs would include measure, cut, align, etc. Unfold the paper. Then draw lines randomly matching nouns and verbs. Write sentences that use your matches. For instance bridge/cut might produce a sentence such as 'The bridge cut the river in two'. An unusual use of verbs often generates additional details.

- Prop up a mirror and describe what you see with specific details. Don't stop with a paragraph. Try for at least a page. Read your draft over—what narrative attitude do the details convey? Dissatisfaction? Humor? Nostalgia?

- Try this same exercise with a dresser scarf, a gift from Grandma, etc. or with one particular object in the room you are sitting in. Circle each detail. Could the writing be strengthened with a better comparison or contrast? Are there any detail connections, a 'boss image'?

Section Four

Photographs

Don't write about man. Write about a man.

– E.B. White

I have a photo of my First Communion with my arm around my brother, Tom, who was a year younger and, even then, resistant to public displays of affection. He stands stiff, frowning off into the distance and I am smiling at the camera, unconcerned by his discomfiture. The picture goes way past a couple of kids on a June day. When that photo was taken, I didn't realize until years later that it told a story about the way our lives would follow that pattern. I was always looking out, he was always looking in.

Photos are an obvious point of reference when writing memoir. Since the camera has been accessible for years, most of us have photos that cover a few generations, especially true if at least one family member wore a camera as if it was an extra appendage. The camera in an instant captures a glance of love (or disgust) or a person looking somewhere else, not a part of the group at all. Those images often express something that you now realize on hindsight, such as that First Communion photo,

Several pictures of a major character in your life can also capture character details. I have a photo of Dad with his hands in the back pockets of his bib overalls. He stuck those hands in his back pockets every time he was thinking or talking or strolling. Without that one image, I might have forgotten a whole string of mannerisms that photo brought to mind. The ways Dad stood, smiled and dressed accumulate and add life to the character I thought I already knew.

The background in photos is also a source of inspiration. A forested picnic spot or a Ferris wheel suggests different stories with the same person as the main character—Dad as hero, Dad with a sense of fun. Most of your photos were probably taken in happy times, but the family picture by the Christmas tree might remind you of other events that happened, perhaps not all happy, that have no photos at all.

Often several photos bring up relationships and anecdotes you have forgotten. A picture of dad and then one of a neighbor—Didn't Dad and the neighbor have a feud over a borrowed hammer? Photos bring those issues to life again. My middle name came from an aunt that I seldom saw and didn't especially like. She wore heavy red lipstick and too much jewelry and she was so afraid of chicken feathers that at first, she wouldn't get out of the car when she and Uncle Walt visited our farm. In my life as a whole, she played a very small role. But there is the chicken feather story, and a few other tidbits that I recalled from a picture of her taken with Mom's sturdy Kodak Brownie.

On the other hand, some photos may never be more than a perplexing inheritance. I have dozens of photos of my parents' cousins or friends never quite connected with me. But before you throw out that dusty shoebox of old photos of people you don't know, examine them for interesting details—the furniture, knick knacks—details that can be used in a family story not about the character in the photo at all. Which brings up an obvious piece of advice: Archive those snapshots you take that are meaningful in your life. Now, with acid free archival materials to keep photos color safe, you can save the images of your family stories and they won't fade away, left in a dusty shoebox without a name. Or scan them, complete with captions, on to a CD that will store those pictures in pristine condition forever. Another memoir writer a few generations down the line will be eternally grateful.

Several photos suggest other aspects of, not only characterization, but narrative form. The girl in that first communion picture that was me certainly couldn't reflect on family sibling relationships or the religious significance of the day. More likely, she was thinking how pretty her white dress looked or that she was the main character. Is your narrative a photo caption or a a bigger story? Is it told as a young girl or an older woman looking back? (More on narrative form in section 9) Photos of the same person in a chronological order, changes wrought by time, bring an altered perspective. Separate photos may not be separate after all, and with some judicious arranging and adding, impressions can be folded into a characterization with texture and resonance.

Finally, the memoir you are writing could include appropriate photos. With a good scanner and printer teamed to a computer, you can incorporate as many pictures as you want. If you don't have the equipment yourself and you want those photos added to a story, get a friend, relative, or neighbor to help out. The equipment is too accessible not to use it.

Characterization

Photo prompts are one way to access a character for your memoir but, whether you use a photo prompt or not, a good story starts with an unforgettable character. Readers love to admire heroes, they love to hate villains, they want to sympathize with the downtrodden, and they want to know what makes the eccentric different. But characters don't appear fully drawn on the page as heroes or villains. They are developed with a careful and conscious choice of techniques that heighten and dramatize.

Character development is achieved in four ways: Appearance, action, speech, and thought. As Kent Haruf said in the *Writer's Chronicle,*

> "All we know about most people comes from what they say to us and what we see them doing; how they walk, how they sit down, how they talk, how they smoke, how they eat, all those things."

In 19th century writing, such as *Madame Bovary* or *Pride and Prejudice*, details of appearance were given a lot of ink. It took paragraphs to describe the heroine's eyes, the color of her hair, and the dress she wore. Before television and films and accessible photography, readers needed such description, but lengthy narrative devoted to physical appearance is now outmoded. Modern readers need only a line or two and they supply the rest from the huge file of images that they've accumulated from the ever-present media. Thus, details of appearance now occupy less page space but, for that reason, need to be selected even more carefully for the right effect.

If the narrator describes Aunt Millie's hat by saying, "Her hat was an impossible concoction of pears and leaves that nodded over her left ear every time she spoke", words such as 'impossible', 'concoction' and 'nodded' characterize Aunt Millie as eccentric. The characterization shifts considerably if Aunt Millie's hat is "a dreamy confection of yellow and green that went perfectly with her spring dress".

With writing memoir, details of appearance are selected to signal your perception of the character. If Aunt Millie scared the liver out of you with her big wavering hat, choose words that emphasize *your* state of mind. Your sister might describe Aunt Millie's hat as that 'dreamy confection', but you characterize the way *you* felt about that hat. Give it all the importance of its effect on you. This is your story and this is your perception.

Details of action set Aunt Millie in motion and say volumes about her character. If Aunt Millie is an angry person; what does she *do*? Let the reader see how she walks, how she treats people around her (tears off her hat, stalks away, sticks her finger in your face). The choice of verbs is important. Does Aunt Millie stride or mince or swing when she walks? Do her fingers jab or shake or flutter? Does she smile or smirk or leer? The choice of verbs will strengthen or detract from the character you are trying to portray. Habits of action also add to characterization, such as pulling on an earlobe, twisting a strand of hair, etc. Repetition of action, if it is not overused, defines character in a "way that reverberates".

"All the world's a stage and all the men and women merely players." (Shakespeare, "As You Like It" Act II, Scene VII), but a character seldom occupies center stage by themselves and keeps a reader's interest for any length of time. Action speaks louder than words, but other people's reactions sharpen the story. Dialogue is also an important element of characterization. Speech can be recorded in summary fashion: Aunt Millie talked about the price of peaches, the length of this summer's skirts, and the Vietnam War with scarcely a breath drawn between sentences. This condensed version is useful in a brief characterization or to get to a core scene, but when the scene is significant in your story, readers feel cheated if they don't hear the whole exchange in direct dialogue: "The country has gone crazy! Youngsters parading on the streets in the most outrageous dress—Some of them are barely dressed at all! Can you believe that these kids know a thing about war!" Aunt Millie's words in quotations are opening up a scene. Somebody has to react to her words.

Fiction writers have it easier than writers of memoir in this respect. They can invent dialogue to dramatize and heighten drama. A memoir writer has to stay on the side of truth, but it's obvious that s/he cannot remember direct conversation, word for word; a certain amount of invention has to happen. As Thucydides explained in his preface to *History of the Peloponnesian War*, "I have found it impossible to remember their exact wording. Hence I have each orator speak as, in my opinion, he would have done in the circumstances, but keeping as close as I could to the train of thought that guided his actual speech." Thucydides wrote when many of our ancestors were still in caves, but he knew way back then that he had to use fictional techniques to bring his narrative alive. You are writing truth, but you can still use the techniques fiction writers pull from their bag of tools. Use dialogue in scenes where you remember the gist of the conversation and the character's verbal mannerisms, such as 'land sakes' or 'would ya believe it'. Dialogue gives the reader a good idea of Aunt Millie's character.

The fourth method of characterization, thought or interior monologue, is even more difficult in writing memoir. You can't tell us what Aunt Millie thinks. However, you can tell us *your* thoughts about Aunt Millie if you are writing Aunt Millie from your own point of view. An ability to report your thoughts in first person point of view is one of the strengths, as well as one of the pitfalls, of characterizing oneself in memoir (In Section Seven, point of view is discussed more fully), but, as I said, seldom does one character on stage keep a reader's interest for long. If too much of the 'I' on center stage sounds flat and passive in first draft, add the appearance of others, such as the Aunt Millie in your life: "I hated Aunt Millie's dress with the big orange flowers. She looked like a walking poppy garden." Or "I could always run like a deer. I was never caught when we played hide and seek. But I was caught at the door. "Where do you think you're going?"

Two additional principles about characterization: First: Never roll a cannon onto the stage unless you plan to shoot it. The character has to have a purpose. This might seem so obvious it is not worth mentioning but, to go back to the photo prompts, you may have started writing a brief caption about Aunt Millie and four pages later Aunt Millie is still center stage. Your writing brought up a reason for Aunt Millie's importance in your life. Why? Before you go on with that second draft, find her purpose in your life. Whoever gets the most ink is the strongest character. You wouldn't have given her so much ink if she wasn't a cannon rolled on to your life stage.

Second: Never roll a cannon onto the stage unless you plan to shoot it. Sorry about the repetition, but often memoir writers feel compelled to write about all those usual landmark events such as 'first date' or 'the day I got my driver's license'. Why? In reality, neither 'first' may have meant much to the memoir writer except that it *was*. In other words, don't write about your first day of school unless it had a purpose in your life, strong and worth the telling. If you report that you played in the sandbox with Shelley and Joshua, it is not a story. But if your experience was a budding realization that altered your life, you will characterize Shelley laughing when the sand fell all over the floor and you will characterize Joshua who helped you clean it up. Did you find out that day that you were a person who loved to make friends and do things with others? Did you find you wanted to be the teacher yourself? Did you love the paint and the scissors and the glue and decide to be an artist? You will characterize yourself and others on that day because you have a purpose in mind.

Whether your initial writing from a prompt develops into a story or a character sketch, characterization still applies. When you begin your second draft, elaborate with appearance, action and dialogue. That first draft may grow into a scene with a purpose for telling—and possibly a series of scenes that are an important part of your life.

The following is a brief character sketch of my dad's mother who was already ninety when I was still a teenager, and I only learned to know a little of her in her last years. I wish I would have had the sense to record her stories in those weekends we spent together.

Grandma Anna

"Grandma, do you want me to fix your breakfast?" I called when I heard sounds behind her bedroom curtain.

"No, no, no, I can fix it myself." Grandma's bent figure came out of the bedroom behind her walking cane. She peered up at me over her steel- rimmed glasses, her blue eyes hardly dimmed by her ninety years. "I don't like the way other people cook my eggs. Rose always cooks them too much and they smell like a chicken coop."

Rose was my mother and when she worked on weekends, I stayed with Grandma. I wasn't always sure how to take care of her though. Stooped and gray and often in pain, the crusty old lady still didn't see why she had to live with my parents or why I had to be around at all.

Grandma made her slow way to the bathroom. Without closing the door, she took down the two braids coiled on either side of her head and slowly unbraided and combed and redid her ancient hairstyle. Occasionally she would let out a little groan, but I knew better than to offer help with this personal toilette. "My hairs are getting thinner every day," she announced patting her iron-gray head as she turned away from the mirror. "Once my hair was thick like yours, but I never cut it. You girls today bob all your hair off."

She came out of the bathroom and continued, "Women are different now. In my day we kept all our body covered."

I hid my feet in flip flops and shorts under the table. She got the eggs out of the refrigerator and sliced a piece of bread for toast. "Once when I was baking bread, your grandpa came in from the field and looked at me with my sleeves rolled up, and told me to roll them back down. He said my bare arms were exciting him too much."

39

I laughed and she chuckled too. I loved her deep warm chuckle as if it came from somewhere deep inside a happy memory. "Yeah, no kidding," she affirmed scrambling her eggs over the hot burner. I watched in fascination as she dumped them on a plate. They looked barely warm. "Do you want some breakfast?" she offered.

"No thank you," I replied hastily. "I'll just have some coffee." I went to the coffee pot and poured each of us a cup.

She sat down and laced her coffee with a liberal dose of milk and sugar. "You should wear good shoes," she said, ignoring my bare legs. "It doesn't do to be walking around half barefoot. You gotta train your feet. You got nice ankles like me. Your sisters all got ankles like their mother."

As the weeks wore on that summer, I learned to bring over sewing or reading for the times Grandma wanted to sleep or just be alone. She was elated to find that I was making my own baby clothes. "That'll make you feel there's really a baby coming," she approved and she would pat me on the shoulder with her tiny worn hand. "You work on those baby clothes and I'll go say my rosary. Then I'll look it over and see if you're doing it right." She would certainly tell me what I was doing right. She had pieced dozens of quilts and had taken on sewing for others back in her day, and I didn't doubt that her sharp eyes would still notice uneven stitches as easily as taking in flip-flops and shorts.

Then the house would be quiet with only the clock ticking and the tea kettle murmuring on the wood stove. My little boy would kick inside me (Grandma told me I was carrying a boy), and when I would look into the living room, Grandma would be asleep on the sofa, the rosary wrapped around her hand with the wedding band, so worn now it was only a thin thread of gold around her finger.

As fall and cold weather approached, Grandma's years as a farm housewife asserted themselves. She got her flower garden ready for winter, stooping slowly but persistently, and chopping, mulching, gathering seeds. It was a small garden outside Mom's porch windows, but no one dare touch it. Grandma peeled apples for the freezer too and one Saturday, she permitted me to help her, although sometimes she would tell me to peel thinner. We sat in the warm kitchen and, over the ripe smell of the fruit, she told me stories of the apple orchard of her dad's, then about the farm she and Grandpa had next door to her dad, how Grandpa (her husband and my Grandpa) had put up their barn, and when he came in and died on the sofa with a horrible headache, and she cooked for weddings and sewed and kept the farm with the help or her two preteen boys. Her hands worked slowly but competently as she told her stories and when Mom came home and saw the apples put away for winter pies, she said that Grandma always worked circles around everybody, and she still could.

One day when I got there, Grandma was already working on a box of her belongings. She lifted a heavy quilt from the box, teetering a bit and I rushed to help her with it.

"I'm going to give this to you and Dale," she said spreading it across the sofa. It was beautiful, dark squares alternating with bright reds and blues. I was almost afraid to touch it.

"Oh Grandma! It's beautiful!"

"It's a log cabin quilt," she said. "I pieced it years ago, but I don't have any use for it. You two living in that new house and it ain't even finished. You'll need something nice and warm." She chuckled. "Even hot blooded young people can get cold you know."

I hugged her gently so as not to hurt her. "Thank you Grandma."

"Well I've got to do one thing. We always put covers on these, so you could just slip it on and off like a pillow case and wash it. I'm going to make one of those for you."

"Grandma, I can do it," I protested.

41

"I want to do it," she said. "Someday when I'm dead and gone, you'll look at this and maybe remember to say a prayer for me."

"Don't talk about dying," I said.

"Why not? I turned 91 this summer. I've been ready to go for a long while, but Saint Peter must not be taking very good care of his books. And when I go, I want all of you to get a keg and dance on my casket. Because I'm going to be up there dancing like I did when I was a girl."

Grandma lived to see my baby boy. "Cuddle him when he cries and leave him alone when he doesn't," she said patting his cheek, "and he'll be a good baby." Then she said softly looking down at his small face, "They break your arms when they're babies and they break your heart when they're grown. Once you start the job of being a mother, there's no quitting."

I wrote this several years ago and found it in one of my old journals with a photo of Grandma. The character sketch is actually a composite of several weekends when I stayed with her. I'm not entirely satisfied with it. The dialogue was pretty close to the actual way Grandma talked. She didn't talk much about her philosophy of life. Her statements were direct and often in the form of a command and usually involved how things were to be done. After all these years, I realize that I was responding to the independent woman she still was inside, a spirit that didn't correspond to the little stooped figure that ignored the little gasps of pain that sometimes escaped her.

I could only characterize her by action and dialogue, since her action and dialogue were toward me. In the original draft, I took out big chunks of my feelings as an expectant teenage wife who just wanted to spend weekends doing what other girls my age did. The chunks I took out needed to be deleted (journal rantings), but now the piece lacks power and focus. I submit it as an example of work that may eventually fit into a bigger chapter in my story. To reiterate what I said earlier, it's important to find the bigger purpose and probably the bigger purpose was embedded in those journal rantings I had to delete. Now it captures the essence of what I remember about Grandma, but I have not yet found where it belongs.

Photo Exercises

- ☙ If you have grown children, use their photos (their birthday pictures, fishing trips, graduation snaps, etc.) to make an album of their history. This makes a good Christmas or birthday present, and possibly a way for them to pass on their own stories.

- ☙ Make a photo collage of you. Cut and paste photos so that they fit the way you see yourself. Include other items, such as drawings, souvenir tickets, etc. that reflect important times in your life. Mount on poster board and use as your memoir cover.

- ☙ Make a picture gallery of your ancestors. Find an old window frame with several small sections. Paint or decorate the frame and arrange pictures of your forebears.

- ☙ Draw a portrait from a photo. Frame it and hang it on your wall or scan it into your memoir.

- ☙ Make postcards or greeting cards from a collage of photos. I make Christmas cards for my children using a collage of the pictures I've taken throughout the year: Paul on skis in January, with a fish in June, by the barbeque in July, with his deer in November. Inside the card, I compose some verse (usually pretty bad) about his year as I see it.

- ☙ This is nothing but mischievous fun and probably should not be attempted without extra copies of a photo. Cut and paste Grandpa's face on your son's body. Cut and paste Aunt Millie's mouth or hair onto your daughter's photo. I cannot say I've found any interesting genetic echoes with this activity, but I surely have had some interesting new characters!

Characterization Exercises

❧ Write a caption for a picture of Uncle Ben, or Aunt Millie. Take into account what is in the photo. Extend the caption into what you remember about Uncle Ben or Aunt Millie that is not in the photo.

❧ Use a photo to start a family story even if you never use the photo in your final collection. A thousand words are worth a picture (to inverse the old adage). You may find inspiration from a photo that's not worth keeping otherwise.

❧ On the other hand, your whole memoir collection can be arranged around family photos. You can write a story about each person in your photo file and it may be your whole family story if you have enough of the right photos. If you have several of a person over several years, each photo can illustrate a life in different stages.

❧ Take several pictures from the same time span and shuffle them and lay them down and see what connections Uncle Ben and Dad had at that time in your life—or Aunt Millie and Mom! Or Aunt Millie and Uncle Ben. Invent a dialogue between the characters that stay close to who they are.

❧ Find one detail in a picture—a purse, a flower—write from that detail into a bigger picture of a character.

❧ Describe your hands in a half-page. Read your description and decide how they have characterized you: Artistic? Hard working? Nervous?

❧ Write a scene about a woman going into an abortion clinic without ever mentioning the clinic. Or write about a man who has just come out of combat without mentioning the combat. Or invent another dilemma that involves writing about a character without mentioning the dilemma. Why? You will decide what your character DOES in extreme circumstances that may or may not be in their belief system. (They do not tear their hair out or faint, but they DO something that expresses their dilemma.) This exercise will strengthen your ability to characterize by appearance and action. In your life, you have seen people you know and love go through extreme circumstances. You have gone through extreme circumstances yourself. Now try this technique with a scene from your own life.

Section Five

A Drawing or Painting

We get from the work an artist's emotional set, the affirmation—even if he doesn't wish to make it—of his eye's relationship to things.

– John Gardner

Kimon Nicolaides in his introduction to *The Natural Way to Draw* says "The impulse to draw is as natural as the impulse to talk." This impulse developed early, long before the written word had appeared. Witness the cave paintings in Altamira, Spain which date back to Paleolithic times. Young children recapitulate this urge to picture a story. As soon as they master the basic shapes, a circle becomes a face, a rectangle a house, a triangle the roof and squares the windows. And then these pictures become a story. The young artist lives in the house and the square represents his bedroom window and the floating face becomes Dad in the yard. The story a child tells from his cryptic drawing is so much more than a sum of its parts, an "eye's relationship to things".

My own interest in drawing and painting came alive the same time in my life that writing did, although I didn't know anything then about the 'multi-modal impetus for artistic expression', education's jargon for the way people often express themselves creatively in more than one way. Tony Bennett's art equals his singing talent, and Zweig's biography of Balzac comments that if Balzac had put his mind to any of the other arts, he would have been as successful as he had been at writing. Even we of lesser talents than a Balzac or a Bennett have probably decorated our phone messages with doodles. I know that several of my writing friends are talented amateurs in music or the visual arts.

Interest in the other arts often stimulates writing and vice versa. A painting or a drawing might inspire a story—or often when I am writing a story, I sketch in my journal to strengthen my feeling for a place. I saw the same thing in my granddaughter. When she was in the third grade, she decided to write a Halloween book about witches. She drew a map of the main road and the witch's house, situated at the end of a crooked trail. She sketched in houses and trees and so on. She didn't spend time worrying whether her drawing was art. She was using it as a vehicle to ground her story.

In one of our adult memoir classes, we used our own sketches as a writing prompt, much as I'm outlining in this section. One woman sketched her mail-box and the story she wrote from that simple drawing was four pages long. Two people brought in paintings they had done of their homes. They wrote family stories that went far beyond what was in the paintings and their stories were so much richer because they were in a firmly-grounded setting.

Drawing focuses on images your eye has observed and your mind has recorded, and those images come back as you attempt to reproduce something as simple as a mailbox or the floor plan of your childhood bedroom. Whatever memories are brought up by the physical act of drawing, there will be a 'bigger picture' behind the sketch. Even if you consider your sketch an artistic failure, the very act of drawing prompts a whole set of additional memories and emotional responses that have been buried for years. I suspect that poets who write longhand before committing their poems to the keyboard are accessing memories and emotions with the physical act of pencil on paper in much the same way.

Drawing as a writing prompt is not a new idea. Wally Lamb, author of *She's Come Undone*, made his own comic books when he was young and still draws to pull him through writer's block. Although he writes fiction and his process is more about story boarding, which will be covered in the next section, he said that his comic book drawings reflect his themes of people in jeopardy.

I know that some will insist they cannot draw. Far be it from me to drag someone kicking and screaming into the realm of the visual arts. I will only quote Betty Edwards in *Drawing on the Right Side of the Brain*:

"...drawing is a skill that can be learned by every normal person with average eyesight and average eye hand coordination."

And Nicolaides, in his *The Natural Way to Draw*, adds,

"As a rule, we learn to talk through a simple process of practice, making plenty of mistakes...but without this first effort at understanding and talking, it would be foolish to attempt to study grammar and composition."

If you are interested in strengthening drawing techniques, I highly recommend either book. They approach drawing with serious purpose, but not the jargon that scares people into thinking that the visual arts are for the talented elite.

Art appreciation is close to the heart of most writers. When you gaze on a painting or a sculpture that moves you, you know that it came with a lot of hard work and revision. The process is the same. And sometimes other's works of art resonate and remind us of a time or place as if the art was created from our own memories. I once wrote a complete short story from a photo of a woman during the depression.

Following the next section on setting are several exercises that will encourage you to use your pencil and journal as a visual artist. Try them. Relax. Have fun.

Setting

Whether you sketch in your journal or paint in watercolor or oils with all the added context of color, visualizing form creates setting in the mind's eye. Many modern short story writers stage scenes in a generic place—an apartment, a street, a car—with nothing to set apart that home or street or car from any other. I suspect it is to effect 'everyman', so the story will not be seen as 'Southern' or 'Midwestern', but in my opinion, this minimalist effect is often boring or confusing or both. Fortunately, more writers than not, emphasize the value of strong setting. Stuart Dybek's fiction and E.B. White's essays both make luxuriant use of setting and their work is strong and evocative.

As we write, we often take place and time for granted. We know the landscape so well and remember the time so vividly that we skip putting in the details that intrigue the reader. At MidMichigan Writers' Conference in October of 1999, Stuart Dybek said it wasn't until he had moved away from his neighborhood in Chicago that he realized those surroundings he had always taken for granted gave his stories originality and freshness.

In teaching third graders, I learned the same thing. When I told them stories of my childhood, suddenly they were *quiet* and then asked questions about a milk pail or what it was like to run to an outhouse in January. They live in a different world, and they liked my stories for big differences in setting from the world they know.

Setting includes time, place and mood. If you start a section of memoir with the heading "July 4, 1967", that date will never make an impression unless the reader hears the music, sees the Fourth of July parade, protestors and all, and feels bell bottoms drag on platform sandals. The reader wants to be there with all his/her senses. You probably are beginning to see that well-chosen details are indispensable to writing.

In a broader sense, the style of house, a description of neighborhood, even certain traffic patterns add to time. If Grandmother's braided rug or Aunt Millie's shag carpeting are details of a setting, these details put the story in a specific decade. But look for interesting time dissonances which can add to characterization discussed in Section Four. What if Grandmother is the one that has white carpeting and Aunt Millie makes braided rugs and refuses to have a telephone in the house? "Aunt Millie stumbled over the braided rug in the hallway" or "Grandmother glided over the white carpeting" are two different pictures of the characters in reaction to their time. Time dissonance contrasts the time and place you are describing with the bigger world. If the time details don't fit the expected, that's dissonance. The rug details that signal time also say something about Grandmother and Aunt Millie's characters.

Time in a story works on more than one level. The memoir writer pens the story at his/her desk, probably writing in past tense and yet attempting to convey to the reader that s/he is in the 'now' of the story even if it took place fifty years ago. In addition, the narrator may interject memories or scenes of another time, not in the story time at all. Often we write, unconscious of the tricky juggling we've done with this time element. But sometimes a writer drops the ball by including a detail from the now into that past world or goes into a memory from another time without signaling the reader that the story has jumped somewhere else.

After you edit your first draft, construct a literal time line for the piece. Does it happen in one day? One week? One month? Block 'now' scenes and put them in the middle, the 'now' of the story, those scenes when the writer/narrator goes from one scene to the next without interruption. If you find scenes that take the narrator back into the history before the story, block those and put the left side of the time line. On the other hand, several reveries ahead of the 'now' story go to the far right.

An example: You are writing about your daughter's wedding. That's the story in the middle of your time line. Then you bring in your own wedding, you write about the disastrous wedding of your sister, you remember your grandmother's story of her wedding. All of these memories go to the left on the time line. Or your story has extended reveries about the upcoming wedding of your neighbor's daughter, your plans for your first grandchild, or your thoughts about getting the house put back in order after the wedding guests have left. That all goes to the right of the story.

A time line alerts you to your story's time flow. Most stories have some of this backward/forward motion. One or two arrows in either direction indicate that the main story is probably still firmly rooted in the right time frame, in which case the time line will alert you to those transitional words and phrases the story needs to signal the reader to a time change. But if several arrows point to the left, the story comes before the story you are attempting. Perhaps the time-lined story is actually the final development of events that happened earlier. Or perhaps it simply reminds you of several other memories that happened after the wedding. A time line that is too heavily weighted on either side of that central story probably need storries of their own and should be cut and transplanted into new soil.

Time is important to setting, but place sets a story so that it "reverberates with…a number of generalizations the author…does not need to make," as Burroway says. A New York apartment and a Midwestern farmhouse are definitely an important distinction. Even though a reader needs to know the geography of place, a lengthy narrative about exact location often deadens the effect. If the rug is an important part of the scene or story, Grandma may have ordered it from the only flooring company in Mooretown, Michigan, or Aunt Millie chases all over Manhattan to find the right material for her braided rugs. Place description depends on well-chosen details. If a story starts with people in action with their setting, location can be established without lengthy narrative.

Setting also sets the mood and tone of a story and can be accomplished with more finesse than with a heavy handed "It was a dark and stormy night..." Find words that establish the feeling you want to convey. If Grandmother's house has a wonderful country setting, you might say, "The silver-gray cupolas towered above me in the autumn sun and looked like a place where a princess might live." However, the mood of wonder can be destroyed with a few wrong word choices. "The cupolas were cobwebbed and gray" may very well be true, but that sentence does not have a sense of wonder and may convey 'neglected' or 'haunted'. Setting mood stays consistent with well-chosen words that follow the 'boss image' mentioned in section three.

Because setting works at more than one level, do not overdo it. To reiterate, if every object is given the same attention to detail, the reader will be overwhelmed and your story will lose focus. Invest the boss image with the importance that it has for the story and use other details of setting to reinforce time, place or mood.

A strong setting is important in writing memoir. We construct our lives from our childhood surroundings or, if our early experiences were hurtful, we construct our lives far away from those surroundings. But our core person developed from a real-life setting. We might like to think we are self-made, but we are where we came from. This goes beyond basic physical setting of course, but the house you lived in, your neighborhood, the school you attended, are immensely important in your memoirs and should be given the narrative that is their due.

This piece came from a diagram of the bedroom that I shared with my sister.

The Room We Shared

No matter what Arlene did to that bedroom, nothing ever fit right. I didn't have any voice in the way my sister rearranged the dented white dresser or the double bed with the painted headboard, first on one side of the room and then the other. Once she even put the bed right in the middle of the room, which worked for me, because then I had a side of my own. I hated it when the bed was against the sloping ceiling. I was stuck on the far side with no way to get out without crawling over her, which was like crawling over a grizzly bear with a sore tooth. At any rate, I could have told her that her efforts were hopeless. Because of the sloping ceiling, the whole north wall was useless except for one big trunk that Mom had stored in a corner.

Arlene tried other decorating tricks that she saw in teen magazines or 'Good Housekeeping'. Her war with our small bedroom continued until she graduated from high school and took her poufy skirts and saddle shoes from the closet, covered with a flowered curtain she had stitched in home economics, one of her favorite classes. She made the curtain wide enough to hide my side of the closet too, a nest of wire hangers that fell between my shoes or the shirts I hung by a button hole on the few hangers that clung to the clothes pole. If that trunk had a flat top, I'm sure she would have covered that too with one of her decorating projects.

She made curtains that matched the closet's curtain for the one tiny window that opened to the front porch roof. It was a window divided into four tiny panes by white wooden slats. and n the summer we took it out and hoped the wind wouldn't come up overnight. Otherwise, bad weather would blow rain on the dresser covered with Arlene's makeup bottles, hair-brushes, and a jewelry box that she watched like a she-hawk watches her nest. Arlene did have some jewelry that interested me, although white clip-on earrings the size of a robin's egg would surely be noticed on my skinny brown ears if I ever dared try them on. I didn't have a jewelry box of my own, or any jewelry for that matter. My stories and drawings of a Mexican knight, Francisco, who resembled Zorro and my drawings that I thought were as important as Picasso's wouldn't fit into a jewelry box. They took up a whole drawer of a brown chest of drawers that Arlene and I divided equally. I often wished that trunk was empty.

The only thing that occupied our room that was never an issue was that trunk in a corner under the sloping ceiling. It had all of our sister Lillian's belongings in it. She had been older than either of us and was killed in an auto accident when I was four years old. Neither of us ever looked in the trunk. I don't know why my curiosity or Arlene's impatience with furniture never overcame Mom's command to leave that trunk alone. But neither of us ever got into it. Arlene and Mom are both gone now, and to this day, I don't know what was in that trunk under our sloping ceiling.

Details play an important part in this setting. The bed, dresser, and chest of drawers were the only furniture, besides the trunk of course, and the reader gets the idea of a 'socio-economic status' (the home-made curtain across the closet, the dented white dresser and the brown chest of drawers that didn't match the other furniture).

There are three points of dissonance in that very short piece (Revisit section two on revision). The bedroom's physical dissonance was that sloping ceiling that rendered a whole wall useless in a small room. Then there was the dissonance of the two girls who shared the room. The trunk, as I see it, was the biggest dissonance of all, the last remains of a dead sister, a bigger, unspoken issue than the arrangement of furniture or girl wars about their standards of orderliness.

No, I didn't plan to say all this. To go back to first draft, those details of setting came out, and that trunk under the sloping ceiling emerged from a simple little drawing, and it had the biggest message of all—two girls living in the same room with the mementos of a dead sister and the untold grief of Mom. I never saw that until I wrote this piece.

First draft. Discovery. It works.

As you use the following exercises with your drawing pencil, and devise exercises of your own, there may be one or more pieces that you will continue to work on because you have found more. That trunk in this short piece loomed larger than I realized. Go back to the writing process in section one and finish the piece using the steps to revise and polish. You may not have a full story but a narrative of discovery which can stand alone in your memoir collection.

Drawing Exercises

- Draw one detail in the setting of your neighborhood, school, or the street where you lived—such as the mailbox I mentioned earlier. You will be surprised that you remember a dent or the crooked way it stood as you begin to draw. Write about that one thing you drew and mention every detail you remember. As you write, the one item will connect with other parts of the scene that you haven't even drawn.

- Draw a diagram of a room in the home of your childhood. Describe the room objectively as if you were a camera recording each detail. Then rewrite with details that convey the room in either a positive or negative light—Or try both.

- Draw a place or a person from a photo in your family album. You may not be pleased with what you produce, but your hand will notice details in the picture your eye might have missed. Write from your drawing, as if you were a stranger looking at the drawing for the first time.

- Draw a scene or a detail from your life with exaggeration— your family home as gothic castle or lumber baron's mansion, the tree by your bedroom window as a noble oak or a wild demonic creation. Use your drawing to write a scene in exaggerated style also. This exercise will get you writing about a setting with strong mood.

☞ If you use watercolor, oil, acrylic, or colored pencil, use exercise three and/or four with the colors that express a setting. The palette you choose may be somber or sunny. It's your perception.

Setting Exercises

☞ Make a list in your journal of all the settings you could describe in detail: Places you've lived, places you've traveled, places where you've worked, etc.

☞ Pick a place from your list. Write a few paragraphs that tell the reader year and place without ever mentioning either.

☞ Pick another place from your list. Write a few paragraphs about it as if it was the best place in the world. Then write about it as if it was a place you never want to see again. Put in particular words of weather, vegetation, colors, anything that will convey the mood.

☞ Write about your home or your place of work from somebody else's point of view—maybe Uncle Harold has come to visit and is seeing your house or your workplace for the first time.

☞ Write a page or two about a place that never existed. Remember time, place, and mood. Read it over and see how many details you used that came from somewhere else in your life.

☞ Read and reread a story you wrote. Highlight each detail of setting. Are there too many? Not enough? Are the examples detailing place? Time? Mood? Are they characterizing anyone? Not each detail will be doing all, but you're getting good when they're doing more than one.

Section Six

Story Boarding

I start at the beginning, go on to the end, and then stop.

– Anthony Burgess

The previous section on drawing segues into this one, but the purpose of storyboarding is different. Basically, it's 'shorthand in drawing' for what happens in a scene, an act, or a whole production. People in drama use it, people in journalism use it, Wally Lamb uses it to kick start his fiction—and memoir writers can use it too. Story boarding resembles a comic strip; a few short sketches outline characters, dilemma, and solution and focuses on action. The short balloon sentences teamed with a simple drawing leave no room for lengthy description or flashbacks. Each frame moves the story forward in giant steps. It is the bare bones of plot, the action of a developed story, with necessary details of difference and body language. It's that story in the middle of a time line with no embellishments.

Divide a journal page into four to six squares. I will not attempt to instruct you on the art of cartooning; in all truth, I don't even have expert advice to give you, except the little I learned for plotting purposes. Draw stick figures even if you have to do weird bodily contortions in front of a mirror. Let's start with a stick figure of Uncle Fred in his kitchen. Fill him out with one or two individual characteristics—bushy hair, thick eyebrows, the most outstanding features of his physique. Draw a straight line for a kitchen counter and add Uncle Fred's canisters that look like ducks. Draw straight lines for his table and sketch in a pile of undone dishes and unopened mail. In other words, sketch Uncle Fred's differences, not his similarities to every other uncle. You may notice that details again play a part in story telling even in an abbreviated comic strip form.

In square one, Uncle Fred gets right to the story problem: "I want to go duck hunting, but they won't let me go to the duck marshes anymore". An active pose illustrates the balloon dialogue. In the next square, Aunt Millie comes in and says something to heightens his ire. She takes it for granted he's more helpless than he is. Next square: Uncle Fred stands up and roars for his car keys. Last square: Uncle Fred out on the duck marsh. In that simple four-picture pattern, you have effected a whole plot with a beginning, middle and end. The restriction of those limited number of boxes clarifies plot. There is no room to get lost in digression.

Those sketches may leave Uncle Fred's story in your memoir as pictured, a simple series of drawings to capture a single vignette retold over the kitchen table or a campfire: "Remember after Uncle Fred had his stroke and went duck hunting anyway?" Or it may be the story board that puts a beginning, middle and end to a family story you remember in much greater detail and deserves a full story you invest with the power of prose.

In my first attempts at story boarding, I discovered a secondary reason for the story board. At first, the body in action took all my attention. I moved my arms and legs and torso in a mirror and tried to make my stick drawings match the contortions I was trying to draw. I had never paid so much attention to body poses before. As I struggled with my crude drawings, I tried to remember how I literally *moved* through my life. When my kids went out the door, did I put a hand on their shoulder as I do with my grandkids? Did I stand with fists on hips, arms akimbo, as my mother did when she contemplated the messes of life? Memories of body language flooded me. I remembered the way son Jim ran, his body as straight as an arrow with only his legs moving faster than sight. Or son Paul's little saunter when he was young and tried to act like a 'big man'. In that first four-picture comic strip, I had effected a whole meditation on movement. I eventually liked what I had drawn enough to include it in my memoir scrapbook.

You may discover that you want to use drawing as an important part of your memoir, whether you use occasional drawings to enhance your written words, or express your whole story in graphic form, similar to a graphic novel.

Plotting

Life Concerns in Order of Priority

1. Life/ survival

2. Health

3. Security (religious, monetary, societal)

4. Prestige/ status/ relationship

5. Sensual stimulation (food, sex, music, etc.)

6. Mental stimulation (reading, conversation, etc.)

7. Suspended action (rest, sleep)

When one inverses the order these priorities in life, there is conflict. Example: Man gives up health for something that will give him prestige.

I introduce this chapter on plot with a list of life priorities, because many, if not most, stories come from an individual's inverted order of priorities. How many of us know someone who puts sensual stimulation over health? How many of us know someone who puts prestige over security? These priority inversions create a 'story problem' and this is the material from which movies and novels are made. Yet those same inversions are what we often see in ourselves, our family and our friends. We are surrounded by stories as good as or better than the ones the media gives us.

We are all acquainted with basic story structure: As Anthony Burgess says in the quote at the beginning of this section, "I start at the beginning, go on to the end, and then stop." We tell each other stories in just this way all the time. If you are telling your friend you went to the grocery store, slipped and fell in the parking lot and sprained your ankle and ended up in the emergency room, you recount the beginning, middle and end in a short time. If you leave out important details, you can elaborate and dramatize the story with humor, danger or pain when your friend asks the right questions. You don't have that luxury with a written piece.

Some stories capture our interest and hold it to the last sentence and other stories, such as my preceding example, sound like a grocery list. How does a story teller keep the listener or reader interested? E.M. Forster says that a story is "...the chopped off length of the tape worm of time...a narrative of events arranged in their time sequence. 'The king died and then the queen died' is a very brief story. 'The king died and then the queen died of grief' is a plot. The time sequence is preserved". A story with plot is a narrative of events, the emphasis falling on cause and effect. In other words, the queen dying of grief implies several scenes of grief taking a bigger and bigger toll on the sad queen (Refer back to the second example of story critique in Section Two for a diagram of cause and effect). Note that falling in the parking lot or the first example of "the king died and then the queen died" ignore the inverted order of life priorities. A story with scenes and plot follow cause and effect, and causes are often result of life priorities that are askew.

The classic structure of story plot is the Freitag Pyramid, loosely diagramed as a jagged pyramid that rises to the story's big, definitive scene (the climax) and then falls off rapidly into the resolution. The beginning, middle and end scenes have to be, not only in the right order, but heightened and presented so that the cause and effect unfold with tension. If the queen dies of grief, each scene brings that cause one step closer to the final effect. The scenes rise in dramatic conflict until the climax and a balance (denouement) is achieved. This plot structure might seem contrived in a memoir, but whole stories that hold interest follow the Freitag Pyramid in some form.

But how do you find a fully plotted story or book from your own life? Michael Holroyd describes research for his memoir *Basil Street Blues*:

"As a biographer, I seek—through familiarity with the letters and diaries, through visiting the places the subject inhabited, through meeting people who knew him—a sense of intimacy that is lacking at the beginning of my research. With my own family I trod the same route but from the opposite direction…"

Holroyd did research, and in so doing, found a story. Holroyd is a literary detective and he knew that a strong element in any investigation is a character's motive. In knowing your character (even if it's yourself), you will find what motivates him/her. I repeat, often motivations are based on an inverted order of life priorities, which puts in motion a chain of events that are cause/effect. Even that example of falling in the parking lot, which looked like an unfortunate accident, might be much more: You're not watching where you're going because ____. If the character was really *you*, how would you end that sentence? Answering the 'because' opens up possibility for a bigger story.

Fully-plotted stories that capture interest are stories of an inversion of life's priorities. As I said in the section on characterization, *story* has to have a purpose. Why are you telling this story? Since I've used poor Aunt Millie, let us continue with her. After writing a first draft, you decide that Aunt Millie is important in your memoir because you discovered your mother's sister has disturbed life priorities that Mother has always instilled in you. The whole story will accentuate this reason, this purpose for telling.

The first paragraph, the first sentence instructs the reader how to read the rest of the story: "Aunt Millie's appearance on our doorstep that April day was a surprise to everyone, especially Mother." What does this sentence do? It tells the reader that the family, including the narrator, does not see Aunt Millie very often. It gives the reader a little setting (that April day) and it gives Mother an importance in the story's plot. 'Appearance' and 'surprise' are the two words that bring a tension, a dissonance to the opening sentence. Everything in a well-plotted story down to the sentence has a tension of sorts, a dissonance.

Each scene also has a rise and fall of tension. In the first scene, Mother tries to find out why Aunt Millie is on her doorstep and Aunt Millie pretends it's only for a visit—the tension rises. Mother knows something more than a visit is afoot, but she ends the scene with set-tling Aunt Millie in the spare bedroom. The scene closes with a drop in tension, but leaves some part of the dissonance unresolved: Mother tries to get information, Millie refuses to give information.

Between scenes there may be transitional narrative—how Aunt Millie spends her first days, the things that tip off Mother why Aunt Millie's really there. Scene two heightens tension. Mother confronts Aunt Millie with a piece of evidence and Aunt Millie confesses she's seeing another man but she's not sure she wants to leave Uncle Harry. She needs time and space to make up her mind. Mother does not want to give her either. The scene closes with Mother giving her a time limit and the tension falls a bit, but the dissonance is heightened.

In scene three, Uncle Harry shows up on the doorstep, the climax, with all the drama you can muster, and then he and Aunt Millie make up and go off into the sunset (the denouement).

You have constructed a memory in classical story form. The raw material from your life is a matter of arrangement along the line of the Frietag Pyramid. There are no hard and fast rules about how many scenes a traditional short story has, but three or four are typical. Story boarding these scenes will give you a plot diagram of parts of the story you choose. What you throw out is as important as what you leave in.

You might be thinking that it's easy to plot a short story pattern with fictional characters, but real life isn't like that. In real life that's not the end of Aunt Millie and Uncle Harry's story. Of course not. In family lore, the brief story might be 'Remember the time Aunt Millie was on the outs with Uncle Harry and she stayed with us for three weeks?', a 'chopped off length of the tape worm of time' as Forster says. But for you, it was a strange time when you realized there was a twist on your perceptions of family, carefully nurtured by Mother. To go back to the purpose of story, this was an important slice of your life and therefore worth giving it drama and tension inherent in the clas-sical story form that has always been the provence of fiction writers.

In a story such as Aunt Millie's in memoir, the purpose of the story is a realization in the narrator. Janet Burroway explains that often a plot line is more subtle, less 'spiked', if you will, than the Freitag diagram: James Joyce saw it as "a crisis action in the mind, a moment when a person, an event, or a thing is seen in a light so new that it is as if it has never been seen before. At this recognition, the mental landscape of the viewer is permanently changed." This defines the 'perception shift' in the critique guidelines.

With Aunt Millie's story, I've outlined a fiction in a memoir writer's life that lends itself to all the drama of the elements of the Freitag Pyramid. Every family has such dramas occasionally. But often the stories in our lives are less 'spiked'. Scenes, stories, whole essays are built around something as small as picking up a stone, driving to Grandma's, or catching a fish resonate because ordinary people go through these personal epiphanies, these perception shifts, all the time. Someone we thought was a friend drifts away and one snowy night when we try calling that person, we suddenly know it's a one-sided friendship. A grown child tells you that he won't be there for Christmas, he's got other plans, and you realize that your child is no longer 'your child'. Epiphanies—realizations—These are the quiet dramas in our lives as we grow and the world changes around us, and they deserve a full treatment, even if the tension doesn't spike. This is the stuff of our stories.

This is chapter six from the memoir of my mother's story which takes place in 1913 in Beaver Township, a small rural area in MidMichigan, populated by Polish and German farmers. Rozia is my mother's name and Beattie is a pet name for a classmate neighbor, Beatrice Trombley. This chapter details the last year of Rozia's school years.

Cherry School ended sixth grade as it did every spring with a program and a box social. Each young lady brought decorated boxes with a lunch for two packed inside, and their box was auctioned off to the highest bidder, who not only had a tempting lunch, but also the company of the young lady who made it. To add to the fun, the ones who bid on the boxes didn't know whose box it was until after they won it. Of course, as often as not, word about who decorated her box with which frills was whispered around.

In other years, Rozia paid little attention to the box social since it was for the big girls. One school program when she was barely out of her chart year {first school year}, Rozia wore Tata's huge fur coat and sang "I am the Robber Baron" and everyone screamed with laughter. She had no inclination to be the focus of that kind of attention this year. But Beattie pulled her into getting ready for the day and as they fixed their boxes together, Beattie was full of conjecture about which boys would bid on their offerings.

"Will you really eat your lunch with Stanley if he buys your box?" Rozia asked, sticking a second piece of fried chicken into her's. Lucky for them, Beattie's mother had chicken left over from Sunday dinner.

"Of course. Stanley's nice. And I know who wants to eat lunch with you too."

"Oh Beattie! Who?"

Beattie's brown eyes danced. "I'm not telling."

The May day dawned bright, and robins and wrens caroled from the trees all the way to school. It was a great day to be alive. Miss Lindsey was grateful for Rozia and Beattie's early appearance and put them to work setting up a table in the best section of the schoolyard under the elm tree and arranging the offerings as the other girls arrived with boxes decorated with ribbon and buttons and beads of every color. As nervous as she felt, Rozia couldn't help but notice how pretty the display looked.

The whole neighborhood turned out for the occasion. The older neighbors watched with amusement as the boxes were bid on and handed out amid squeals and blushes from the young ladies and swaggers from the young men. When Miss Lindsey finally held up Rozia's box, decorated with pink and white crepe paper, Rozia felt her face grow hot. What if no one bid on it? Verna's box went unbidden and Mr. Ratajcyck bought it to the laughter and cheers of the neighbors.

Rozia was surprised to hear from the back, "Fifty cents."

"A dollar," someone responded. Rozia was afraid to look around and see who was bidding. When her box finally went for three dollars, the noisy audience cheered and clapped when Joe Gorsky walked up to claim his prize.

"I'm not going to eat with Joe Gorsky," Rozia fumed to Beattie, who sat next to her, serene in the knowledge that Stanley had bid for her box.

Beattie turned and giggled, "You better, Rozia. Some little birdie told him whose box that was."

"You didn't!"

"I never said I did now, did I?"

When the bidding was over and the buyers and sellers found places around the yard and in the trees to sit with their feast, Rozia hid in the schoolroom that was set up for the afternoon's entertainment. The desks had all been pushed against the walls and extra chairs brought in for the neighborhood audience.

Out the window, Rozia saw Joe finally sit under the elm tree and open the pink and white box by himself. She felt terrible watching him, but she couldn't sit with him. She hardly knew him. What could she say? What would he say? She just couldn't.

The day was a long one for Rozia. After the lunch and entertainment, there was an ice cream social. For once, Rozia was almost happy for Verna's clinging company. When the shadows were long and the birds were singing their evening song, people began to drift away.

"Stanley's walking me home," Beattie said as they helped Miss Lindsey put the schoolroom back in order. Rozia could tell from her tone that she was not happy with the way Rozia had acted. Rozia nodded without comment. She would walk home by herself then. Even Verna had already left.

But on the schoolhouse steps, Casimir Stodlowski, approached her. He was a big, burly young man, already out of school. "Can I walk you home?" he asked.

Rozia was taken aback. Why would Casimir want to walk her home? She hardly knew him.

"I bid on your box too," he said.

"All right," she agreed. Perhaps it would atone for her rude behavior to poor Joe, who had disappeared from the festivities as soon as possible.

They followed Beattie and Stanley, and Rozia watched them enviously. They were singing songs from the entertainment, their voices floating back in a surprisingly good duet, occasionally punctuated with a burst of laughter. They seemed to be having a lot of fun.

Casimir talked little.

"Do you know any of those songs?" Rozia asked hopefully.

"No. I never did learn too much at school."

Rozia fell silent. He didn't even sound embarrassed by his admission.

The evening had turned to dusk. The robin that had a nest in the doorposts of Steve Nowak's abandoned store, sat on a branch of a nearby tree and scolded them.

"Let's sit down on the steps and rest a minute," Casimir said, looking up and down the road. Except for Stanley and Beattie's figures disappearing into the evening light, the road was deserted. Everyone else had already gone home.

Rozia sat down by him on the old wooden steps, wishing that the walk was over.

Without warning, he grabbed her and bent her back on the porch. His big body pinned her down and his mouth, coarse and hard, was on hers so that she felt she would choke. In a surge of panic, she pushed against him.

"Quit wiggling," he snarled, and his hand fell on her leg.

"Beattie!" she screamed. "Beattie!"

"Shut up!" he said and clapped his hand over her mouth. She dug her nails into his hand and tried to kick him.

She heard running footsteps and Stanley's voice. "Casimir!"

Casimir let go of her and Rozia scrambled up from the porch, pulling her rumpled dress straight.

"Get the hell out of here," Stanley threatened. "What kind of person are you?"

Casimir didn't answer, but turned and walked off in the opposite direction.

"What's the matter with that dirty thing?" Rozia fumed, pulling once more at her dress. She felt as if she had smudges wherever Casimir had touched her.

"Are you all right?" Beattie asked.

Rozia's face flamed under their concern. "I'll be all right," Rozia said. "He's gone. Go on. I'll be along."

There was no sense in spoiling Beattie's time with her new beau. She followed her rescuers at a discreet distance the rest of the way home. Would Stanley tell everyone about Casimir? She thought back and could see nothing that she had done, but she felt as shamed as if Casimir's attack was her fault. How would anyone know what she had or hadn't done? She had seen and heard the big boys snigger and talk about girls before.

Tears of frustration and helplessness burned her eyes until she could hardly see the two lovers ahead of her. She thought of Joe. Joe would never have attempted what Casimir had done. How wonderful this last day of school had started, and how dismally it had ended.

At this point, my mom's story in its entirety is with an editor. I struggled to make each story in our taped interviews a chapter in her long life, but it wasn't easy. Even though the stories she told me had a purpose for being (this story the end of her school years), none were embellished with detail or emotion. They were "just the facts".

Nevertheless, most of her stories had the bare bones of a plot. At this point in Mom's story, the significance of her choices that day dramatized her lack of self-confidence and laid the foundation for much of what was yet to come. It took many hard life lessons before she learned to assert herself. My own realization, as the writer who rearranged Mom's stories into chronological order, did not come until I had written (and eventually rewritten) the chapter in a plotted format.

The chapter has three scenes: 1. Rozia putting her box together with Beattie (dissonance: Who knows about Rozia's box?) 2. Day of the box social (dissonance: Joe Gorsky bid on Rozia's box and she won't eat with him), 3. Evening walk with Casimir Stodlowski (dissonance: Casimir attacks her and she has to be rescued by Beattie's beau). Within each scene, Rozia's lack of self-confidence drives the story with cause and effect. If Beattie hadn't instigated putting a box together, Rozia would have ducked the issue, if Rozia would have honored Joe's bid, she wouldn't have been left isolated at the end of the day, if she hadn't been isolated at the end of the day, she wouldn't have fallen prey to Casimir.

In spite of Mom's sparse narrative on tape, the scenes are accurate, the dialogue was close to what was actually said, and the setting details were embellished from later research and my own imagination, but still true to my mother's story.

Story Boarding Exercises

- ∞ Make a list of 'short stories' in your family repertoire. Frame them as comic strips. Check the ones that are story boards for a more fully developed story.

- ∞ Look at one of your journal entries. Find a point of dissonance, even if it's a small one. Look at the preceding events of the day and how and if the dissonance was resolved. Why was this part of your day dissonant? Did your motivations clash with someone or something else? How? If it's 'someone' else, he or she has motivations too (But if the washing machine flooded, you can't impute a motivation unless you want to have fun writing about your malevolent machine). Frame your journal entry in a four-frame comic strip.

∾ Stand in a full length mirror. Act out how you felt throughout your experience in number two. Exaggerate. Can you see a plot pattern emerging (shock, reaction, acceptance)?

∾ Take notes on stories you are reading or watching on TV. Is it an inversion of life priorities? Are the secondary characters helping or hindering the main character? Can you capture the plot in a four or six frame comic strip?

∾ Use the Life Priorities list to look at your own life. When and how did you invert priorities and what happened? Story board your discoveries.

Plot Exercises

∾ Take an incident with some dissonance from your journal and write it as a scene. Write at least two pages. Can you extend it by writing what happened before this scene? Can you divide what you've written and make two scenes out of one?

∾ When you've completed the first draft, look at the first sentence, the first paragraph. Does it give a hint to the reader what the dissonance in the story will be, the first paragraph 'hook'?

∾ Take a marker and draw a box around each scene. You may find that you can't tell where a scene starts or ends. You may find that you can't find scenes at all. You may find you only have one full scene. That's the value of this exercise.

∾ Pretend you're a movie director who's looking at each scene as something that will be acted out. In your revision, be sure you have action and tension in each scene.

- Read several memoir pieces from different sources. Bracket scenes, look for transitional material, try story boarding one of the stories. Was the epiphany in the character's actions or in the narrator's observations?

- Describe an important event in your life—a birth, death, wedding, etc. Write in one sentence your personal realization from this event. Would anyone else reading your journal entry come to the same conclusion?

- Write the same event from another character who was in the scene? Is there different tension? Is there a different realization?

Section Seven

Letters

*Even people who are reticent to talk about themselves
can't help telling others about events significant to them.
It's as if nothing has happened until an event is made
explicit in language.*

– Roger C. Schan

In Curtis Cate's preface to George Sand's biography, he remarked that at least 19,000 of her letters have so far been inventoried, but he says,

> "These figures, though impressive, are not as monumental as they sound. At a time when the telephone did not exist, it was not uncommon for people to write two, three, or more letters a day."

Cate constructed a 730 page biography drawn from Sand's letters (for interested readers, George Sand was a woman, who adopted a male pen name and was the mistress of Chopin).

To examine Cate's statement about the importance of letters, biographers of those who lived before the 21st century, had a rich source of material. The Founding Fathers wrote letters (unfortunately, George Washington and Martha's personal letters were destroyed by mutual agreement, to the sorrow of later generations), generals wrote letters, writers such as Henry James wrote letters, kings and queens wrote letters. And ordinary people wrote letters. The Pony Express, trains, boats, and later airmail carried letters across the country and across the world before the instant communication of the Internet..

My generation may be the last real letter writers. Before my computer and email, I wrote letters incessantly, although not to the extent of a George Sand. In the seventies, there was a small magazine called 'Lex', which published a list of those who wanted to correspond with others. The lists were coded by areas of interest and subscribers were worldwide. At the time, it scratched my itch to write, and it was so much more rewarding than writing to publish. With letters, I *always* got positive feedback. I had pen friends from all over and we exchanged poetry, philosophy, postcards, photos and stamps.

When I read them, it's like looking back at old journals, except these are wise and witty responses to my concerns back then. If you were a letter writer who saved letters you received, the collection is a mirror that reflects a past time of your life and all its concerns through another's eyes. If biographers can use letters to write another's life, I should be able to use my letters to construct my own memoir, although that mirror may not always reflect an image that is flattering. For example, I have a letter from my older sister chiding me when I was around twelve years old. Mom went on the first vacation of her life, and I was complaining that I had to handle all the kitchen chores. When I read that letter now, I cringe at my young self-centeredness, but I also remember how much I missed Mom's presence in the kitchen. I might have forgotten that time if I didn't have my sister's scolding letter.

You might use a letter written years ago and respond with a letter written from where you are now. Now that I remember the feelings that masked my complaints, and although my sister is gone, I could write her a different letter than the one I wrote when I was twelve, a letter that better expresses the more complex feelings I didn't know how to express when I was a preteen. You can use the letter form to talk to those in your life that you want to remember. In these letters that are never delivered, I can direct sorrow, rage, joy, and nostalgia—all the emotions that I never expressed in the moment. A whole memoir collection could be in letter form.

Even if you were not a letter writer yourself, you might be able to track down letters that other members of your family have written.

Letters are an invaluable asset to family history and the viewpoint of your ancestors that made that history. And they are written documents that can be quoted directly.

Letter writing is probably not a lost art—just a changing one. You might start a family or friend's round robin letter even if it is by email. Responses accumulate as each adds to the letter until it comes back to the one who started it. It's a good way to compare others' perceptions of a character or event especially if the originator of the round robin letter poses a central question to be addressed.

A special kind of letter writing is a collaborative letter journal. When our family spends a week up north together, we each write a letter in an 'up north' journal and later we contribute pictures. Since we've been doing this for several years now, our 'up north' journal is getting quite thick, and it's obvious that each of us has our own special memory of the same place and time. I smile every time I read this entry by a nine-year-old friend of my granddaughter's: "We went to some lakes to find the guys fishing and we about got killed by my mom driving. We finally found them and it was pouring and me and Leah jumped out, trying to catch frogs."— Abby. I remember that evening down horrible two-track trails to get to those 'secret' fishing spots the guys teased us we could never find. Abby evidently remembers the drive also, but the scenic wilderness was not what she noticed when we got there. It was those tantalizing green frogs at the water's edge. Round robin or collaborative letter writing could also be used to gather thoughts and memories on the birth of a child, a graduation, or the death of a loved one.

Point of View

Letter writing is a special kind of prose. It has a certain form, and is usually written with an expected response in mind, and is always written from a personal point of view. After discussing plot in the preceding section, an explanation of point of view is appropriate here. Janet Burroway says,

> "Point of view is the most complex element... a question of relationship among writer, characters, and reader"

There's a reader on the other side of the written word, and point of view not only greatly changes the distance between writer and reader, but dictates word choice and character presentation. Journal entries or perusing letters often give a memoir needed information. A writer may even choose to write a whole narrative in letter form (Writers such as Samuel Richardson wrote epistolary novels, whole books in letter form. His most well-known is *Pamela*). Whatever form you choose, that conscious decision brings up the question of point of view (POV) and will greatly affect what the writer wants to accomplish.

A story can be written in first person (I watched Aunt Millie cross the street), second person (You watch Aunt Millie cross the street), or third person (She watched Aunt Millie cross the street). Even in these brief examples, you can already see a difference in perspective, as if looking through a camera and changing the focus of a zoom lens. Each point of view has its advantages and disadvantages, but each point of view offers a "different relationship among writer, characters, and reader."

The first person point of view puts the narrative and the character in close proximity to the reader. When fiction writers write in first person, the 'I' narrator, is *not* the writer, although the story's narrative is cast as if it was. As Henry James said, it's an eye on "that accurst autobiographic form which puts a premium on the loose, the improvised, the cheap and the easy". He was not flattering to first person point of view. The good news is that memoir writers have the right to disagree with Henry James and go on to prove him wrong. The bad news is that it is not easy to prove Henry James wrong.

Of course memoir writers are often likely to write in first person but a first-person narrative can easily fall into "that accurst autobiographic form which puts a premium on the...cheap and easy". Example: Jane comes over for coffee and tells me (with all the story teller's elaboration) that she was in the grocery store and pulled a can from a display and the whole pyramid crashed and rolled all over the floor, I will listen to her story with a) impersonal interest, b) amusement, c) sympathy, or d) boredom. What colors my reaction?

a) Interest: If Jane tells me her story in a straight-forward way and includes what she knows about setting up store displays, details that extend my knowledge, and the flaw that caused the accident, I end up with some interesting information. Jane's story is nonjudgmental, a bad experience in a busy woman's life. b) Amusement: If Jane recounts the cans rolling every which way, people jumping, stock boys running about, the store manager's red face, we will both laugh at the scene. c) Sympathy: If Jane's unfortunate move hurt the little old lady behind her with a rolling can, I feel her concern that she was the cause of someone else's misfortune. d) Boredom or animosity: Jane has taken center stage of her own pity party. The stock boy's reaction was angry, the manager frowned at her and the checkout lady was rude- it wasn't Jane's fault that the display was in the way of her cart. By the time Jane is finished with this tale of woe, I am probably on the side of the others involved in her story.

With this example, I have covered several ways that a first person's story might sound. Even in fiction, establishing the right relationship between reader and writer in first person point of view is not easy and with memoir, it becomes doubly difficult . In relating stories that are your own, a shield of defense arises. No one likes to cast themselves in a negative way, especially if we imagine our employer or our mother reading our words. The way you tell your story in first person, that voice, that tone, can sound 'whiny', 'self-indulgent', or 'aggressive' with the wrong word choices (more about tone or voice in the following section). Readers put themselves in a story, and no reader wants to identify with a character such as Jane in example D. If your first-person point of view story shares interesting information, if you naturally see the humor in situations, or if you see the 'otherness' in people or things around you, you will probably negotiate the autobiographical form without appearing 'cheap or easy' as Henry James characterizes it.

Another downside of using first person involves what the writer/ narrator can know. The narrative cannot go outside of what the 'I' character experiences firsthand. Secondary characters can only be characterized by what the first person knows or can observe from their actions. This may not be problematic in memoir unless the story includes a grandmother or uncle that takes up a lot of space in the memoir. With such stories, the 'I' needs to step back from the story (The story I offered in the section on characterization had this problem).

A third person point of view may work better. Third person, 'he' or 'she' for matters of convenient categorizing, can be divided into third person limited or third person omniscient. A third person limited voice reports all that happens through 'his' or 'her' eyes and mind. Third person limited stays with 'he' or 'she', and their setting, but it gives the writer more latitude and the narrative voice an opportunity to adopt a tone 'apart': "Henry decided it was time to clean the garage. He was not the kind of man who let indecisiveness take up many corners of his life. When he made up his mind, neighbors saw his garage lights burning at three in the morning, and heard the garbage can ring and thud with discarded objects he once considered important to keep. If his wife was dismayed the next day at the bare garage, he felt no remorse. It was the easiest cleaning job he had ever done." Notice the narrative voice. It conjectures and notices everything around Henry in a separate voice.

Third person omniscient achieves even greater distance, what I term 'God's eye'. This point of view sees all that is going on with everyone. In one paragraph the reader sees what Henry is doing and thinking, but the narrative does not necessarily stay with Henry. In the next paragraph, the narrator dips into the neighbor's thoughts and actions and into the garbage collector's recollections, and so on.

What third person point of view gains in objective narrative, it loses in distance. The 'I' point of view is up close and personal, and brings a reader quickly into a close relationship with the charater. Third person, especially third person omniscient, causes the narrative to adopt an 'observer' stance and the writer has to work with word choices to keep that distance from feeling cold and clinical.

The second-person point of view, 'you' is seldom used for extended narrative, although Jay McInerney wrote a whole book of fiction, *Bright Lights, Big City*, in second person and caught the attention of critics for that very reason. As I write this book, I often lapse into the second person point of view. 'You' are my audience, my class, my writing buddy across the kitchen table. "You Sister" and "First Love" were written in second person point of view and I think that decision came from a personal need to address both my sister and my ex-husband in this point of view, similar to the narrative voice of a letter, an explanation to myself and them about the way I felt at that time in my life. It is also why those pieces are short. I couldn't have maintained that point of view for long without sounding shrill or pedantic. Second-person point of view has a finger-pointing quality and can get too close, too preachy. Try it on with a short piece of narrative, but beware. It's personal (much like writing a letter), intense and hard to use in a book-length narrative.

In writing memoir, you might wonder why you need to consider the second or the third person point of view at all. It doesn't seem like the way to write memoir. As Clarice Lispector said, "What others get from me is then reflected back to me and forms the atmosphere called 'I', Her stories were about that reflected 'I' that forms the perceived atmosphere of an individual, whether the perception is accurate or not.

However, especially with short memoir pieces, you may need to use other points of view in writing about significant characters in your life when you were in fact the observer. And sometimes emotional pieces that you cannot write in first person may work well in third person. At first it might seem strange to write, "She grew up on a small farm in Michigan" when the 'she' is you, but it might give you the emotional distance to tell your story with the objectivity that didn't work in first person.

Point of view is a conscious decision, the way a writer focuses a story through a character. Although memoir seems to demand the first person point of view, the decision depends on the effect the writer wants to accomplish. You may find that adopting other points of view comes easier than the 'accurst autobiographic form'.

The following is a found poem (described in section eight) written by a poet friend, Chris Lucka, who used a letter from her aunt for the text. In using this form, she escaped the 'accurst autobiographic form' to capture the character of someone she loved and admired.

Aunt Esther's Letter

She writes on note paper
with paintings of early Americans—
Ogala Sioux by Daniel Long Soldier
or chooses cards with paintings,

"Summer Days by the Sea"
with a young woman
overlooking the ocean edge,
a lighthouse on a long land finger
poking into the sea.

Today she writes
"We're now having some very cold weather.
I picked Boc Choy, lettuce and dahlias
before the frost comes.
I saw a gray heron in the flood control chute
on my morning walk near Myrtle Street.
Yesterday I saw a big tiger cat
carrying a squirrel
under the dogwood bush
by my raspberry plants.
I'm reading *The Beans of Egypt Maine*
by Carolyn Chute. You'd like it I'm sure.
Ellen gave me tomatoes.
I'm processing eight pints today.
Our class is having our 58th reunion
at Swift River Inn near Cummington.
It's a lovely place. I plan to go.
I hope to hike Mount Greylock
for the Ramble on Columbus Day.
Ron and I went to Northhampton Fair.
We sat in the bleachers and it rained.
I won two perfectas on a big grey mare.
I'm cooking trout for supper.
Tonight is hymn sing at church.
I'll take Gert.
Sunday we'll have a covered dish supper,
also the big Foliage Parade in North Adams.
I went for a swim at Bellvue Falls last Sunday.
It's getting cool.
Take care and enjoy your trip to Boston.
Love Esther".

Even though this example is not prose, I offer it as an example of an artful way to use sentences or phrases from several letters compressed into found poetry, a point of view that would have been far different if Chris had chosen a first person narrative to describe her aging aunt.

Boc choy, dogwood bush, big tiger cat are details, specific names. Chris arranged the vividly descriptive phrases and sentences in chronological order and captured the essence of her aunt, a very lively, active older woman. Yet the selection closes with a line that illuminates the subtext of age: "It's getting cool." That final poignant line is of course commenting on the end of the summer season and the arrival of autumn, but it is also a reminder of the human cycle of life.

I borrowed Chris's idea to revisit my own overflowing file of letters. The character of letter writers became accessible for me without wading through files of letters hard to read in their entirety. In addition, I added photos, poems and postcards into a memoir scrapbook that I cherish.

Letter Exercises

- ✆ Write a letter to a famous person in history and describe your life in the 21st century in light of that person's character and accomplishments: 'Dear Abe, Since the Civil War..'

- ✆ Write a letter to the author of a book or film that influenced you and describe how and why it was important to you.

- ✆ Construct a letter of advice that someone from history would send you.

- ✆ Write a letter to someone you care for and say all the things you may never have told them.

- ✆ Write a poison pen letter to someone who deeply upsets you and air your grievances. This might be a good one to throw away later. You could also write letters to characters in the news who are politically corrupt, pompous, or otherwise flawed.

- If you have letters (or maybe emails?) from someone important in your life, try found poetry or a prose description, using phrases or sentences from their own words.

Point of View Exercises

- Choose some incident in your day. Write a paragraph about it in each of the four ways described in the preceding ''Jane' example. Notice which one of these paragraphs feel like the easiest to write.

- Pick an object or a group of disparate objects such as a key, a spoon and a candle. Write for ten minutes about the objects using first person point of view, ten minutes in third person limited, and ten minutes in omniscient point of view. Read aloud what you have written and notice how the change in point of view changes the narrative distance.

- Write a story about yourself in third person: "She did not want to get on that big yellow bus, and if it wasn't for Arlene's firm grip, she would have turned around and ran back into the house."

- Write about a scene in your life as if a camera is recording it. Call yourself "the girl" or "the woman" (a la Hemingway), as if you didn't know anymore about yourself than the camera.

- Write about your most embarrassing moment, your worst moment, and your rottenest thoughts. This is to prove to yourself that you are not the perfect hero(ine). Nobody can identify with a character that is too good or too bad. Good writers of memoir write about themselves as if they were writing about a character they know, warts and all. This is very hard. If you can do it, you are truly another Frank McCourt and you will probably write the next *Angela's Ashes*.

Section Eight

Music

He simply tried to translate into sound the soul's cries...

– Pierre d'Alheim (on Mussorgsky)

Next to vision, the sense of hearing is our most powerful sensual mode. Imagine the cosmos without sound. Imagine your life without the voices of those you love. Imagine the silence of a world without music. Some of the first sounds of your life were lullabies and later nursery jingles. Then there were first songs you learned in school and the hymns you learned if you went to church. Whether you are an avid lover of music or not, you were imprinted with the rhythm and pattern of music as early as you were imprinted with the rhythm and pattern of speech.

Every culture has an archive of music we all learn at an early age, from the A-B-C jingle to the national anthem to holiday standards. Music lends powerful texture to our lives more than we realize. Marketing experts realize it. Many commercial jingles become as familiar to us as the songs we learned in preschool, and the sound tracks that play in shops are setting a mood to buy the merchandise on display.

When I began using soft music to enhance my attempts at meditation, my goal was not related to writing at all, only to stop those spinning mind wheels that tend to clutter my head with static in the normal course of my days. It wasn't long before I found that as I drifted with the music, filaments of memory, little memory snapshots, floated up unpredictably. Often I abandoned my efforts at meditation and grabbed my journal to describe the color and texture of barn rafters or the smell of an alfalfa field. The power of 'neutral' music to stir random memory was surprising to me. I learned from my own experience later that many writing instructors use music to induce a meditative state to encourage that first free-write phase of a writer's process described in section two.

For some, music is a time especially set aside just for listening and appreciating that special symphony or opera or the music from 'Miss Saigon'. For others, music is the sound track that accompanies their daily lives. I have a considerable collection of music that is an archive of personal memories, that sound track of my life. "Summer Place" reminds me of the summer I met my husband and brings back the feel of summer sand and the smell of hayfields. "Green Door" brings back my first high school dance and the magic look of the gym with muted light and classmates 'dressed up' (I know I'm dating myself with these examples). Music from the past can put you into the middle of a love affair, into the middle of pleasure or into the middle of pain and brings up a strong emotional response that has nothing to do with the technical worthiness of the piece. The way that music affects us goes deeper than an appreciation for a certain musical genre and pulls at our memories as strongly as looking through an old photo album, whether the notes and rhythms come from a guitar wired to a speaker with infinite decibels or a solo violin.

Tom De Marchis said in the "Writer's Chronicle,"

"One could argue that a piece of music is a narrative form unto itself, taking the listener on a journey similar to a written narrative..."

De Marchis interviewed several writers and found that each had a certain musical ritual to enhance their writing. Stuart Dybek listens to jazz when he composes, Robert Olen Butler listens to Beethoven and Brahms. If rock music makes you feel alive, country makes you cry, classical makes you feel sublime and anointed, jazz makes you feel in control, use the rhythm, the "journey similar to a written narrative" to enhance the mood and mode of your written words.

Just as a reader adapts to the differences in fiction or biography or history, so a writer can use different musical genres to heighten the mood for each particular piece. The writers DeMarchis interviewed edit with different music or no music at all. They used music to enhance the mood of the writing they do. In editing, they needed the cold eye of objectivity without the effect of that particular music. DeMarchis' findings resonate with the writing process discussed in section two. In the first steps, we do all we can to access the freewheeling creative part of our mind, even though, in the final steps of the writing process, we do all we can to work with that cold eye of objectivity.

Narrative Voice

When Mary Karr in *The Liar's Club* tells of growing up with an alcoholic erratic mother, I hear a young girl's voice full of innocent honesty tell a story that would make any parent shrink in horror. When Ruth Reichl (*Tender at the Bone*) tells her story dealing with a manic depressive mother, her ironic, adult humor overlays her story with tough survival. Both are stories of growing up with a dysfunctional parent, yet the voice of these two memoirs is very different and very honest.

Your writing voice, if it resonates as honest and believable, might be compared to the particular style of a musician. Not only do we recognize the difference between jazz and country music, but lovers of jazz know Coltrane when they hear him, and country aficionados recognize Johnny Cash or Willie Nelson in the first line of music. These musicians have strong, distinctive voices that are their own. Even though aspiring musicians may learn technique from the masters, the technique has to be adapted and transformed by their own voice. Those who try to do the very same thing as Coltrane or Johnny Cash just sound like second-rate imitators.

Voice, style and tone are often words that are interchangeable when it comes to talking about how a writer 'sounds'. A good writer's voice is as strong and distinctive as a musician's—Dickens, Faulkner, Hemingway are some classic examples. But how does a writer capture the tone that lures a reader to know and trust that voice on the written page? What makes you—an ordinary person with a normal life—sound strong and distinctive on a page like a Mary Karr or a Reichl?

There's an old Irish story about a writer coming through the pearly gates and Saint Peter stops him. The writer braces himself. He knows he has not always done right and he expects Saint Peter to ask, "Why were you not more like Christ?" Instead Saint Peter asks, "Why were not more like yourself?"

To 'know yourself', borrowed from Greek wisdom, is now a cliche, but there is no other way to express that simple truth. However, with the written word, I will give you an example that may help in finding your own voice. In looking over my old journals, I discovered several masks that were not my voice. First, I went through a 'pompous' period when I described everything from washing the dishes to a child's birth with the same drama. I used long sentences with as many multisyllable words as I could cram into a sentence. I usually ended these entries with some 'important' moral: "Just as I broke the platter in my haste, so I had broken his heart with my lack of care." I never talked like that in my life!

Then I went through a period of trying on other writers' styles. I tried to sound like every writer I admired, from Margaret Atwood to Thomas Wolfe. Now I can flip open a journal from that period and can tell you who I was reading without going past the first paragraph.

These were all writing masks. I kept trying on someone else's voice. In my defense, Roethke said, "Imitation, conscious imitation, is one of the great methods, perhaps the method of learning to write… The final triumph is what the language does, not what the poet can do, or display." So, perhaps trying on all those masks had some value after all, although I didn't know it at the time. I just thought I should sound like a 'writer'. I took on the voices of the writers I admired instead of looking inside myself, the voice inside my own head that talks to me all the time and never tries to imitate anybody, that 'final triumph of what language does, not what the [writer[can…display'. When my mother used to say in her most exasperated moments, "Who do you think you are?" I should have looked at that question (or exclamation) a long time ago.

Many faults of finding voice possibly come from those English classes that emphasized formal papers meant to practice grammar, organization, all those language tools for basic writing skills. That objective voice has its place, but unfortunately, that style often clings to our written words, a mode of expression meant for a decent business letter, which leaves out individual voice entirely. When the gap closes between formal writing and intentional informal writing, the voice of a writer emerges. I believe many other writers go through that same 'trying on' process I did, finding the gap between the way a 'writer voice' sounds and the way your own voice registers.

So, how does a writer acquire his/her intentional voice that is more distinctive than a high school English essay? First, the voice or tone of a memoir depends on the reason for the memoir. In *Writing Your Life*, Will Stanek says,

> "Tone designates the attitude the speaker (narrator) has toward his subject, his audience, and—especially in a memoir—himself."

The voice of *Mommy Dearest* holds an edge of bitterness. Muhammed Ali says that he is the greatest with a certain bravado that lets us know he is tweaking us. These memoirs follow the voice of celebrity that somewhat dictate their voice.

The chosen point of view, explained in the previous section, adds to Will Stanek's definition of tone as that "attitude the narrator has toward his subject." Most of us, like Reichl or Karr do not have the luxury of a given celebrity 'voice' to tell our stories. To go back to that description of Jane's story, stories come from the attitude the memoir writer has towards her/himself. How does that voice in your head record what 'it' sees? Does it laugh, judge, rage or react with wonder? (If you thought you were the only one who 'talks to her/himself, be comforted. It's a human phenomenon.) Really listen to that voice and analyze its attitude.

Second, the voice of the writer comes from selected details the writer uses in a story. In *Self-Editing for Fiction Writers*, Renni Browne and Dave King give examples of six characters with a similar background, education, and gender. Yet each character's voice is wonderfully different. One notices the green print in curtains and another remembers Mother leaning on a shovel. You may rightly objet that fiction writers have the choice of dozens of narrative voices—a youngster that doesn't understand the world around her, an eccentric woman with a crabbed way of looking at life, a man suffering from guilt—The memoir writer is restricted to the single character, the 'you' of childhood, the 'you' of adolescence or the 'you' firmly anchored in the present. Even though the examples are fictional, memoir writers who write from who they really are, will just as surely pick the images and details that describe the perception of their lives. One may note a shovel and never look at the pattern of a curtain's print (Again, notice the importance of the right details and image patterns discussed in section three).

If your memoir uses an essayistic form to "designate the attitude the narrator has toward his {her} audience", it will be largely narrative. The narrative form establishes a close voice, similar to the way you write journal entries or letters. The reader feels as if the narrator is engaging in a conversation with the silent reader at the other end. As I look at the examples from my own memoir writing, they are largely in this form. Writers who excel in this form, such as E.B. White, use humor and/or wonderful language to keep the reader's attention. Essayistic writers may use techniques that short stories use such as dialogue or minimal plotting of scenes, but their use of short story techniques is more selective.

On the other hand, a memoir such as Mary Karr's *The Liar's Club*, uses short story techniques as outlined in section six and builds the story's message into the climax or epiphany, leaving action and plot to tell the story. If you are strongly drawn to writing dialogue and characters in action, your voice will register with a plotted story such as Karr's.

To compare the two forms to music, the essay form is a solo, such as an a cappella singer, an acoustic guitar or a trumpet playing taps. The audience hears every note. A solo demands perfection from the single voice or instrument. Story form resembles a symphonic piece, such as an orchestra concert or a big band performance. Several instruments work together to produce a unified sound that resonates. In a classical short story several elements work together to produce a work that also resonates.

As Pascal said, "When we encounter a natural style we are always surprised and delighted, for we thought to see an author and found a man."

This part of my memoir collection is possibly one of the most painful pieces I've written. My oldest brother's death was totally unexpected (a car accident), and this came from a few lines I wrote in my journal after I had finished taking care of his personal effects and was listening to some of the classical music from his tape collection.

Burning My Brother

I spend days with a pen or a phone in hand but now the thank you notes are written. The phone calls are over. My youngest brother and his wife help me clean out my big brother's apartment, the small space he lived in for the last fifteen years of his life. I have room in my garage and so everything he left is here—with me—the youngest sister, the only sister left. I am not a trustworthy character. I scare easy, I veer left when I should veer right. I am not like brother Ed. I must have been an enigma to him and yet here I am, the one who will take care of what he left behind.

After we clean out his apartment, I clean out my closets and paint them a quiet blue. I answer my brother's life that remains in piles in my garage with sorting and throwing away reminders of my own. I give my grown children their baby pictures, their school work and photos, extra bedding I thought they might need if they ever came back home again. It is an irrational way of dealing with my brother's death, but it has a logic of its own.

After a few weeks of turning away, I finally go to the garage to all that is left of my brother, a priest, who lived 77 years in the eye of his God. On one side of the garage, he has few personal effects—some clothes for me to sort. They are good clothes. Someone will appreciate the warmth of a black wool coat, the fit of well-made black slacks, black shirts. They don't look like priest's clothes really. Without the Roman collar, they are just good dark clothes.

I sort and give his rosaries and medals to nieces and nephews. They can use an extra rosary or crucifix. Some of them don't go to church anymore, but what can it hurt if they have religious symbols in their lives. We all need reminding that we're part spirit. And it was what my brother lived—belief in the spirit—a difficult way to live where malls sprang up around the little area he served that had once been farm land. He was as mystified by those temples to material needs as others were puzzled by his devotion to his religion.

The other side of the garage is overloaded—files of correspondence, files of ideas, notebooks of his homilies, boxes and boxes of books. I keep a few books, give the theological ones to the dioscean library. And then I tackle his personal files. I go through pages he has written in his fifty years as a priest, file after file on the education of children, the importance of marriage, the decrees from his bishop, the letters from his parishioners. I see this brother, nineteen years older than me in a way I had never seen him before. He had never shared his personal life with any of us, a quiet implacable life, a silent ministry to every human digression. He tried to answer with the burning sword of truth as he saw it. The bishop in his eulogy called Father Ed 'the quiet priest from Omer'. It was the single most significant statement about my brother that rang true in all the flowers and words of sympathy that tried to reach who he was.

As I become acquainted with this brother through his writing, I relive the anguish he must have felt when Mom died the year before, and I wonder if the day he drove his little blue car in front of the sand truck, if he was missing her on that first anniversary of her death like I was. Why did he stop at the stop sign and then drive into that intersection, unless he wasn't really looking at the world of trucks and physical forces, but thinking of the guiding spirit that had been with him for years and then left him an orphan when he was approaching the days in his life that were careful and calculated—time ticking louder and louder with each day? My brother priest, who buried his father and four sisters, was finally mortally wounded by the mother who lived for his weekly visits.

Ed and I were closer in our sorrow when Mom went through her final year than we had ever been in our lives. I had always called him Father Ed since he was ordained when I was eight years old. I wonder now if pasting that 'Father' in front of his name kept him a priest first and a brother never. We had taken our roles without question back then. But in that last year, he talked more about daily events such as going to the doctor and about my petunias. It sounds fairly mundane—but was he trying to jump over 'Father' and just wanted to be Ed?

He kept up visiting every week as he had done when Mom was with us. I should have hugged him when he left, his shoulders beginning to bow, his dark hair finally grayed. He needed a hug and there was nobody to give him a hug but me. But neither of us knew how to erase forty years. I hug acquaintances I haven't seen for a while—and I never hugged my brother who bought me piano lessons when I was in high school and then paid me to play the organ for him, who baptized my children and stood by my mother's death bed with me. I never hugged him. So he's gone now and it can't matter to him anymore.

After two weeks of not living, but reliving his life in those volumes of files, I burn my brother. I stand by the fire pit with a shovel, turning and turning the stubborn paper, the endless words that tried to express the ineffable, the ephemeral. I don't want all these personal files in the garbage I tell myself over and over. I am finishing what has to be done in a businesslike manner. But I feel like Satan burning a lifetime of care and worry and prayer.

The flames are burdened with the reams of tight pages and they flicker and lapse into smoke. I poke them and they flare on a new edge here, a single page there. They consume years of words reluctantly. The air around me is electric with a coming thunder storm. Frogs and crickets fill the darkness with ceaseless sound—the same sound that Father Ed heard on the farm when he did his chores and said his prayers and went to bed—the same night noises that I heard years later when I did the same. Now the sounds unite us while the flames erase the rest.

As I said, this piece of memoir grew from a few lines in my journal, and the first person point of view was already firmly in place. Perhaps because this was written in those first weeks after my brother's funeral, it feels like my real voice. I was too close to my own emotions to even think about how the words came out. I just wanted to say to myself all the things that crossed my mind in those sad weeks. I think that is also why I used present tense—The story was still happening as I wrote that first draft. The voice truly did come from inside with no filters. For you, my classmates, it's an example of how content dictated form.

The form is essayistic. In spite of my inner turmoil that used first person in present tense, there is a forward-moving organization—Deceased brother's personal belongings in my garage, sorting out belongings, (after some flashbacks), burning brother's files. However, I did revise (If I haven't said it before, writing is rewriting). I worked at toning down the 'me' part of the story, even as I knew that the story was mine, since the only way Ed was characterized was my own observation of his personal effects. Conjecture about what my brother thought or felt was the way I dealt with my own grief. There are elements of guilt, of dramatizing the effect of Mom's death that was probably more my own, and an element of family legend in the fact that he was buried the day my mother died the year before—a coincidence too strong to overlook in this kind of narrative. My brother's death may go unremarked by the rest of the world, but to my family, it has to have an importance, a kind of tragic reason.

It is revised as well as I can do it now and, for whatever it is worth, I chose it, because this is one journal entry where I did not try to put on a mask.

Music Exercises

- Make a list of the musical selections you love.

- Write why you are drawn to a selections in exercise one. 'I like____ because'____.

- Choose one selection from exercise one and write about the memories that it has for you.

- Close your eyes and really listen to a selection you love. Use the melody as a meditative vehicle. Then free write everything that comes to you. Don't stop to think. Just write.

- Use a line or lyric from a favorite selection and add a lyric of your own.

- Choose two different musical selections and write a paragraph about yourself, comparing the way you feel and remember with each piece. Don't mention the music in the paragraphs. Do you sound like two different people? Or one person at a different stage in life?

- Choose a piece of current music you like. Free write for ten minutes. Did this music invoke memories? New ideas? What did you learn about yourself, your writing? Answer these questions in writing. It will clarify the connection between a music prompt and your response.

- Try mixing lyrics from two different songs you love.

Voice/Tone Exercises

- Read newspaper editorials or personal essays and label the voice that the narrator sets. Is it ironic, humorous, angry, sad?

- Take the information from an editorial and rewrite it with your own opinion. Does the voice change using the same facts?

- Go back to old journals and letters. Tape a few entries and listen. This is how you your written word sounds—dialect, quirky language and all.

- Look at one of your pieces and give your voice a label. If it is ironic, humorous or folksy, find at least three places where you can change or add a word, phrase or sentence to heighten that voice.

- Read a selection from a published memoir. Compare to selections from exercise three. List differences. List similarities.

- Take a selection from your previous writing. Rewrite in a different voice. If the paragraphs are solemn, recast them in a humorous style. Try writing them as if you are the British nobility or a Canadian trapper. This is an exercise trying on different masks.

Section Nine

Poetry

A poem is a small machine made of words.
When a man makes a poem, he takes words as he finds them and
makes them into an intense expression of his perceptions...

– Randall Jarrell

This section on poetry segues from the preceding one on music so closely they could be folded together. In the days before the written word, troubadours, accompanied with lute or lyre, related news from a town they had just visited or a a hero's exploits with their invented poems. Stories were orally transmitted with rhythm and expression; poetry and music were synonymous. As early troubadours disappeared, written poetry lost touch with the 'farmer, the baker, the candle-stick maker'. Now, schools struggle to introduce written poetry in the classic cannon to students, far removed from the time and place that inspired those words, not a part of that shared community that a troubadour took for granted.

Nevertheless, poetry survives in modern troubadour's garb. Most of those students who can't understand Shakespeare's sonnets or Walt Whitman listen to Cold Play or in my day, Neil Young. Maya Angelo said in a lecture at Saginaw Valley State University that she understood rap. The rhythm, the chanted words speak to a new generation in a new form. Poetry still captures powerful images and emotions from the world poets live in now.

However, this section is neither about poetry set to music, nor about the value of a sonnet or a sestina. Rather, it's about using a poetic form to express yourself in your journal and possibly a way to express yourself in memoir. A poem arises out of a moment in time that, with compressed language, rhythm, and word choices, evoke the emotion of a moment. When you were young, you may have written poems for just that reason and then threw them away as an unworthy attempt at 'real' poetry. Every writer has probably heard the old dictum that if you can write poetry, you can write short stories or novels, because once poetry is mastered, the rest will be easy. It gives poets the praise they deserve. Because a poem is compressed, often expressing a whole scene in a few lines, each word must be the exact word. If a word or a beat slips, the poem falls short.

Such high praise might scare a memoir writer from the possibilities of the form. In this section, I'm asking you to revisit the times you felt the urge to write something short and swift to vent a powerful feeling with an immediacy that cannot be said in any other way. My old journals are filled with scraps of protopoems that I've written through the years and each one was written when I was feeling extreme anger or grief or joy. Although I've gone on to work on some of these lines and even had one poem published, I do not consider myself a poet, yet I value these lines when I revisit them. Though I may not sound like Maya Angelou, some of my poems have a place in my memoirs; another way of capturing a vivid memory.

Assisted Living by Marla Kay Houghteling and *Beautiful Rust* by Ken Meisel are two examples of Michigan writers who have told stories from their lives with poetry, Houghteling dealing with the last years of her mother and Meisel with the changes in the Detroit landscape he remembered. You may not compose a memoir in poetry, as these writers did, but in looking at some of your writing, the preceding sections on whole story may not fit either. These pieces may be between a formed poem and prose—a prose poem.

I hesitate to introduce that term in this section, since it may almost need a section of its own that relates to flash fiction or snapshot pieces. These hybrid styles of writing use compressed language and/or metaphor much as poetry, but the form is narrative prose. By addressing the small, the word count is an asset to concise creativity. "Zelda" could be a prose poem if it was edited and condensed. (Refer back to the writing example in section one on journaling). It was not meant to be a poem, yet in its 'snapshot' prose, it expresses a feeling, an impression similar to poetry. If you have never attempted in your life to write a poem and never intend to, some of your journal entries may resemble prose poetry and can be enhanced with revision.

Poetry is part of our received culture. Once upon a time schools demanded that children memorize and recite not only poetry, but other words of powerful prose that comes close to poetic expression, as part of their education. I'm probably one of few that wish I had that experience. If you have a lover of poetry in your memoir, quote one of their favorite poems. The last time I visited my brother Elmer before he passed away, he quoted Shakespeare's "Tomorrow and tomorrow and tomorrow" soliloquy in its entirety. He was one of the generation of students that committed several such pieces to memory, and the words stayed with him all his life. In my memoir scrapbook, his section ends with those lines.

A poem can be a road map for a story from your own life. Use lines of poetry to introduce a memoir section that mirror the idea in your own story, much as I'm using quotes to introduce the sections in this book, or compose your own couplets to introduce sections of memoir. Read poetry for the inspiration it may give you to write your own story in whatever way you choose.

Even if poetry, in all its myriad forms, does not entice you, the following section on poetic devices will add texture to your writing style. At the conclusion of this section, I've outlined a few very basic forms for the pure challenge of trying to fit a whole thought in exact word counts or beats per line. It can be exasperating, but it's more creative than working a crossword puzzle.

Poetic Devices in Prose

Much in a poet's tool box are the same tools that effective prose writers use. Southern writers are especially adept at using poetic prose. William Faulkner and Flannery O'Connor pepper their stories with unusual and original similes, analogies and metaphors that thrived from a heritage of oral storytelling. The troubadour tradition survived south of the Mason Dixon Line long after more northern American writers had succumbed to the flat prose of the Puritan spirit. However, even storytellers of the northern variety can borrow from the poet's tool box to deepen and texturize their prose.

Poets spend a lot of time searching for the exact word in their writing process, and the 'right' word in the English language is often tricky. Modern English is built on its own Anglo-Saxon foundation and then layered with borrowed words from several other languages, especially French (the history of the evolution of English deserves a book itself). Thus we have a wide and varied vocabulary, rich in synonyms (words similar in meaning), but that wealth can be a writer's pitfall. As Mark Twain puts it, "The difference between the right word and the almost right word is the difference between lightning and the lightning bug". Hence, the Oxford dictionary and the thesaurus are two important items in a writer's basic materials.

Word usage rises and falls in meaning. An obvious example: Early in the 20th century, a writer could use the adjectives 'queer' or 'gay' to describe a character without being labeled a homophobe. Updated dictionaries attempt to keep up. My 1970 dictionary's definition of queer as a homosexual is entry number 6 (the first entry is the oldest word meaning). That one word carried five earlier meanings, and probably earlier writing used every one of those meanings. This is an obvious example of latest usage of a word in our ever-changing language, but sometimes you may use an older definition purposefully. If Grandpa described his neighbor as a "queer, old fellow", that word needs to stay.

Word choice often stumbles on the connotation of synonyms. Connotation is that slippery meaning that is an idea conjured up by the word, aside from its explicit meaning. For instance 'scheme', 'plan', and 'plot' are synonymous in a thesaurus. Yet if you describe Uncle Fred as having a scheme, it has a connotation of being a little underhanded or secretive. If Uncle Fred has a plan, he seems to be logical and goal-oriented.

Before we leave word choices, the poet's toolbox includes symbolic words, words that can stand for a whole set of ideas. Symbols are part of our everyday life. When a journalist writes, 'the White House reported', you know a big house is not talking. The phrase is shorthand for the president and his staff and possibly his whole political party. When you hear the phrase. 'the cross and the sword', the words bring militant Christianity to mind that could take paragraphs to explain. A memoir writer can also use this shorthand. If brother is a tough, outdoors person, 'mountain man' can characterize him and symbolize a whole train of attributes as the story unfolds.

Unpacking the poet's tool box brings up other ways to enhance prose. Some were mentioned in section three on details (Use of details keep making their appearance), such as comparing or contrasting one thing with another. Similes, as the word indicates, compares two nouns that strike the writer as similar, and often use the word 'like' in the comparison: Example: 'Her eyes were like the gray rock I had seen on the Lake Superior shoreline'. Of course, no one's eyes are rock, but comparing eyes to rock expresses not only eye color but an unyielding attitude.. Similes layer meaning and arise from the story you are writing and come into a first draft almost unconsciously, part of a writer's experience. That simile would never occur to someone who has never been on a rocky shore.

An analogy closely resembles simile and infers that, because of structure or function, one thing resembles another. Example: 'Del's dash across the field was as fast and sure as a cheetah's, intent on its prey'. This sentence compares one aspect of Del (speed) to a cheetah. For our purposes, an analogy is very close to a simile, but usually uses 'as' instead of 'like'.

Perhaps the overuse of similes and analogies prompted Ernest Hemingway, that master of concise prose, to despise them, proclaiming that one word is *not* like another. I choose to disagree with Hemingway but beware of the overused clichés that soured Hemingway: 'Her skin was like silk', "His eyes were as sharp as daggers". They creep into first drafts, media seepage. Keep only those that come out of your own life, your own images.

Metaphor is closely related to simile, but more difficult because it demands more image patterning than a simile. By that, I mean a metaphor states that one thing *is* another. If a simile claims that Del is a cheetah, then he has several characteristics of a cheetah. With a simile, you can usually compare and then go on with other character-ization that keeps Del a speedy guy. But if you say Del *is* a cheetah, a metaphor demands that you follow Del as fast, sleek predator. A wonderful examples of a well-done metaphor comes from one of my memoir classes. We were doing the exercise 'I am a ____" and one lady compared herself to a truck. Her one-page description was a perfect metaphor. She roared down the left lane, she made a lot of noise, but she never took anyone else off the road. She described everything she saw in herself in terms of a truck, and everything fit in a wonderfully fresh way. An extended metaphor over the length of a book would be very difficult, but it worked well as that one-page prose poem.

Sound repetition is another powerful tool in a poet's tool box, and underlines importance for the reader. Alliteration repeats the same beginning letter sound of a word or phrase: 'the power of prose' (or prose power), the 'sameness of Samantha (or 'same sassy Samantha'). It is often used with titles or subtitles and used by the media for that reason. In a narrative, it is effective if not overused or used in the wrong place.

Of course, most of us are more familiar with repetition of ending word sounds, rhymed poetry, jingles, and many musical lyrics (Many people still think that poetry has to rhyme). Rhymed poetry has a jagged history. There have been great poems and musical lyrics that use rhyme effectively, but there are also countless others that used forced rhyme or predictable word choices, such as 'June' and 'moon' that brought rhymed poetry into a less favorable light. Ending sound repetition usually works against a prose writer: 'He glowers with power' or 'His nose was like a rose' doesn't make Grandfather's description memorable. On the other hand, repetition of sentences give a passage solemnity and majesty: "Samantha *saw* it all. *She saw* the rise of Derek's company. *She saw* the pain in his wife's eyes. *She saw* etc. etc." However, it is irritating and intrusive if that is not the effect the writer is attempting to achieve.

Finally, the rhythm of sentences is as important to good prose as it is to good music or good poetry. Basic sentence structure is simple and declarative; composed of subject, verb, object: Mother fixed dinner. Harry grew watermelons. That structure has its place, but a string of sentences that follow the same pattern deadens a piece even if it's adorned with a few adjectives. Read and reread your words aloud.

Listen for the balance of sentence length and variation. As a general rule, longer sentences usually involve description or interior monologue. Short sentences denote action, transition. As always, this is not a hard and fast rule, but it's a start. Look at the last word of the sentence. It is the word to leave with the reader, a concrete word, one that evokes an image: "The house I went in" is a poor arrangement of words that uses 'in' to carry the prose forward. 'I went into the house' ends with a concrete noun. Better yet, did you creep, stalk or slam your way into the house? Exact word choices, sentence rhythm are both powerful tools in a poet's toolbox and can also be powerful tools in a memoir writer's toolbox.

If you are an omnivorous reader, you have an advantage here. Reading good prose gives you that ear for interesting word choices and the rise and fall of good sentence rhythm. Lines of Sandra Cisneros's *Eyes of Zapata* have such a powerful rhythm, they almost read like poetry. And again, to use Southern writing as an example, who has read Faulkner and not met with one of those Faulknerian sentences that he could sustain for half a page? Exact placement of words and word markers create a majesty and solemnity to his prose.

Content dictates form. The thought, the feeling, comes first, then the form that best contains the words you have generated. If your memoir is mainly prose, your words will be stronger if you borrow some tools from the poet's tool box. Or you may find that some of your writing is best served with a formed poem or a prose poem. And yes, the poet has to revise, read, and revise again to polish a poem in much the same way outlined in section two—the writing process.

I found both of these poems in my journal, and I probably don't have to explain that the first was written on an almost prayerful note after my mother died. I wrote the second after finding out that a friend was less than truthful. Both of these times were emotionally charged and these entries were written in my journal just as you see them. The line breaks are totally idiosyncratic, but several end on a strong word, a technique often used in free form poetry.

Mother

the unknown,
the unknowing,
Embrace me.
Hold me under your feathers;
the naked chick,
the shivering child,
the fearful, flightless one.
Warm me
until my wings find strength
to spread,
to reach
for the space around you;
the space I learn to call my own.

False Friend

Not a word said out of place, out of context.
Not a word said that could be taken
and held like a diamond, hard and gleaming.
But soft, mushy;
If touched they oozed between the fingers
like swamp slime.
They fell into the room and slid silently
into dark corners.
No one touched the words while they were watched
with the eyes of the one who spawned them.
Those eyes—not the knowing eyes of a cat,
or the wary, evil eyes of a snake;
Not the blood lust of a wolf's eyes,
or the red-eyed anger of a bear.
Wide flat eyes with no light around them.

As I said earlier, I'm not a poet and don't wish to hold up these
journal entries as examples of great poetry, but more as examples of
the way we find symbolic language to express emotions too powerful

to describe in prose. The first used a mother bird image that probably arose from that child inside all of us. The second compares true words to diamonds (cliché!) and false ones to swamp slime and then goes on to look for the truth in the eyes of the liar. I don't know why these particular images arose as I was writing but at the time, they best expressed a strong moment in my life.

Poetry Exercises

- Collect poems you like. Copy, cut and paste (or keyboard them) into your journal. Underline words or phrases that made an impact.

- Try acrostic poetry with a person, place or thing that is special to you. Write a word vertically and find a word or phrase that uses the first letter of each letter in the word. Example:

  Quiet
  Useful
  Interesting
  Love in every stitch
  Timeless

  You might have to look up a few words to finish an acrostic. These words could surface somewhere else in your stories since you've brought them into your working center. Or the acrostic poem may stand on its own as an addition to your memoir collection (I wrote an acrostic for my name which adorns my memoir scrapbook).

- Concrete: Using a shape, follow the outline with words relating to that shape. For instance, you might sketch an outline of your cat and around the shape, use words that describe what the cat means to you.

- Try a Cinquain:

  Line 1: A noun. Name of what you're thinking about (Aaron)
  Line 2: Two words describing the first line (Young, vulnerable)
  Line 3: Three action words (Smiling, frowning, pacing)

Line 4: Four words that tell how you feel (I'm full of love-worry).
Line 5: One word that repeats line one or is a synonym (Grandson)

The cinquain has a nice-looking form when you put it together:

Aaron
Young, vulnerable;
Smiling, frowning, pacing,
I'm full of love-worry
Grandson

- Found poetry: Underline words and phrases that catch your eye in a story, an article, a letter or your journal entries. List them on another sheet of paper or cut them out if that's feasible. Rearrange them so they have meaning and form (example in section seven with Chris Lucka's poem).

Prose Exercises Using Poetic Techniques

- Look at your writing. Do you compare one thing to another (such as the example of eyes like gray rock)? These images surface in your rough drafts. However, they may be cliché or not be as clear or strong as you want. Close your eyes and conjure up comparisons: "Aunt Millie's hat looked like____ (Flanders field in July? A drunken sunflower? A florist's dream gone awry?) You'll know when you hit on the comparison that comes closest to your image.

- Take a person, place or thing and define it by imitating a poem you admire. "How do I love my cat? Let me count the ways"

- Try word-bumping. (This is a good way to generate the words or phrases you can put into a form). Take a noun, any noun. Put a word with it. On the next line put another. Then another. And another.

Example: basket,
brown basket

brown basket, broken
grass basket, woven, etc.

Don't think hard with this. Just keep letting the words bump into another image and the following image bump into the next. You will have a whole list of phrases that might yield one you love and can use (I ended up with 'downy basket belly' which was the right description of my cat). This exercise needs repeating.

∞ Try writing a sentence of 250 words. What does this have to do with poetry? It's an exercise in exact placement of words and word markers that make the sentence understandable.

∞ Put yourself in a metaphor. "I am a ___".

∞ Look in a thesaurus or a dictionary and find unusual words that you like. Make a list and then try pairing your choices with another word: Eccentric Harry—then add phrases explaining why Harry is eccentric…

always late
with never a new thing to try.
He brings ice cream in January
and chili in July.

Section Ten

Recipes

*And so our mothers and grandmothers have more often than not,
handed on the creative spark, the seed of the flower...*

– Alice Walker

Developing a recipe-based memoir has a whole family history
built in—a timeline studded with memories of celebrations that
gathered family around a homemade feast, and the stories that were
swapped over the meal. A memoir centered on food can be as elaborate as Ann Romney's *Family Table*, which includes photos and family stories to enhance the recipes, or as simple as a standard recipe
book with a few notations on the way that recipe came into your file.
Was that creamy dessert an aunt's recipe at a baby shower? Was that
unusual salad a friend's contribution at the last book club meeting?
When I started to put together this section of my memoirs, I found that
I had dozens of recipes from family and friends, written on the back of
envelopes or napkins or torn from pieces of wrapping paper.

Old recipes from Mom and Grandma are bits of history in themselves. Instead of microwave directions, they instruct the young cook
how to hold the temperature steady in a wood burning range and mention brands of baking supplies that no longer exist. Fundraiser recipe
books acquired from a church or a civic group are memory jostlers
also. I have at least a half dozen of these, going back to my days as
a young wife and mother. Occasionally, as I leaf through these dog-
eared volumes, I run across a name of one of the contributors that

brings back a whole string of memories I might have forgotten forever. Whether a recipe reflects a family history or a history of community, recipes have changed over the years. I have a German cookbook with the most interesting old recipes that would make a heart doctor wince.

Hopefully, recipes you may not have used for years have not been discarded even if they fell into a back file. Recipes reflect a family's past interests; the economy one-dish meal recipes that you used as a young mother, recipes for dishes to bring to social gatherings you may no longer attend, or recipes that followed a fishing phase or a camping time in your life. The year my daughter and I came back from New Orleans, it was a gumbo autumn. The year I traveled to Greece, it was a moussaka summer. The year my son worked in Alaska, we ate halibut and salmon every time we got together until we had eaten every single fillet he sent home. Every time I see those recipes, I have a whole string of memories that go way past the simple list of ingredients.

The way we prepare the food we eat, how we conduct meals with family and friends reflect the pocket of culture we live in. Hot dogs and potato salad go with the Fourth of July and summertime family reunions, turkey is traditional at Thanksgiving, a ham dinner and boiled eggs celebrate Easter and the return of spring. You may or may not follow these cultural food traditions, since I am only quoting traditions from my own little corner of the world. If you are Jewish, Spanish, Afro-American, or Asian, you probably have a different holiday menu list, although recipes often reflect the wider culture that touch us. My roots may be Polish American, but my menus also include bagels, burritos, fried okra, and dozens of other dishes borrowed from American diversity.

The traditions that surround food include, not only the food itself, but how and where the meal is served, which involves setting and rituals. Grilling the meal on the deck and eating at a picnic table is a far different scene from Grandma's dining room with silver and crystal. Does your family bless the meal before eating? How? Who serves the food? Who sits where? Why? These rituals have been with the family so long, they are taken for granted by all who belong. Put yourself in the middle of a family meal as an outsider and describe what you observe.

At a meal, plans are made, friendships are solidified, and life passages are celebrated. Recipes may be easily accessible on the Internet, but recipes that hold friend and family stories are in your recipe box, food for countless memories. Kate Christensen, author of *Blue Plate Special: An Autobiography of my Appetites* mentions in one of her blogs, "I'm always disappointed by novels in which the characters don't eat. Fiction without food is like fiction without dialogue". Since Christensen wrote an autobiography centered around food, fiction is not the only genre where she considers food important.

Legends, Myths, Fables and Folk and Fairy Tales

Legends, myths, etc. connected to a recipe prompt may seem confusing at first, but family recipes invariably recall family gatherings, and family stories told around dinner are oral stories that most resemble legends and myths. Just as every culture has its own rituals and special foods to celebrate important occasions, so every culture has its own stories that have been passed down from ancient oral story telling, and the form is as familiar to us as the nursery rhymes and jingles mentioned in the section on music. These ancient tales were usually meant to pass a lesson to the next generation: Industry and patience protects you from life's catastrophes ("Three Little Pigs"), beware of strangers with a power of persuasion ("Little Red Riding Hood"), forgive when forgiveness is asked ("The Prodigal Son"), and use your head to solve a problem that seems unsolvable ("The Thirsty Crow and the Vase"). Even though Asian, African or Native American stories differ in cultural allusions, all have stories similar in content and message. Joseph Campbell, in his book, *Hero With A Thousand Masks*, pointed out that all cultures have mythic variations of one great narrative. His work is well worth reading. Modern poets and prose writers such as James Joyce's *Ulysses* and Steinbeck's *East of Eden* allude to these stories as part of the culture they expect their readers to recognize.

Although several early oral story forms are included in this one section, they differ somewhat in specific purpose, and if this brief introduction piques your interest, I've listed a few sources in the reading list. Parables and fables are short, fictitious stories to illustrate a moral lesson. Fables, such as Aesop's, usually used animals to dramatize the story, whereas Christ's parables involved human characters. On the other hand, a legend was largely believed to have some basis in history. King Arthur may have actually existed, but the stories that grew around him were invented to dramatize valued heroic qualities. Myths attempt to explain a phenomenon of nature, unseen forces that exerted an influence on mankind, although archaeologists are finding that some mythic heroes also have a basis in fact. Perseus may not have slain Medusa, who was reputed to turn men to stone, but he may have been the founding father of Mycenae and the driving force behind its architecture, which, to my mind, is as noteworthy as Medusa's head.

A fairy tale is largely one where magic intervenes in the form of fairies, wizards, witches, etc. Although the hero or heroine is helped or hindered by magic, s/he prevails with human ingenuity and endurance. Grimm's fairy tales, one of the earlier collections, were often a little 'grim', and modern versions leave out some of the more graphic elements. Some creative writers for children have turned fairy tales upside down by telling the story of the Three Little Pigs from the wolf's point of view, or invented stories about what came after "happily ever after".

Folk tales (tales of the common folk) incorporated strands of legend, myth and magic and possess details of the culture from which they came. F.H. Lee in a 1930 edition of *Folk Tales From All Nations* notes,

> "The same essentials recur, but the local setting gives an individuality to each story. This unity in diversity is illuminating. The fascinating parallels that may be traced between the stories told by various races show that there is a basic kinship between nations in spite of superficial diversities."

F.H. Lee had discovered that same pattern of narrative that Joseph Campbell did. For our purposes, it's enough to know that the Cinderella story has 300 versions throughout the world, and there may be a family Cinderella story in your own family history.

In that brief description, perhaps a memoir writer can label the family stories told around a camp fire or dinner table. Uncle Harry believes that his neighbor's house was struck by lightning for a sinful way of life. Aunt Millie's past loves were as heroic as King Arthur's knights. Cousin Sarah has a dozen stories about the good luck of her favorite hat that has saved her from several disasters. The moral of these stories may be askew, but there we are, as human as those ancient story tellers who told tales of Cinderella or Beowulf.

These oral tales have a different narrative than the writing techniques outlined in the previous sections. Details of time and place are blurred: 'Once upon a time' opens a fairy tale, and the listener never knows if the story happened in 1542 or 1998. "A crow was very hungry." The crow's surroundings are never mentioned. Was the crow hungry because it was autumn and the crops were harvested? Only the story's skeleton remains: character, action, result. Often, realistic cause and effect, discussed earlier as an important element in story, is put aside and the tale emerges from another principle that is outside predictable behavior of physical forces. The story's logic hinges on advice from a bear or a stick that points the way home.

Oral family stories that come up repeatedly at family gatherings resemble the familiar myths and legends from our wider cultural heritage. They usually start with 'Remember the time'— and skip setting details much as those old fairy tales. The tale goes right to a family member that encounters a dilemma and acts in a way that illustrates their character and/or family values. One family story that I story boarded for my memoir scrapbook involved daughter Annette and Rebel, our lovable hound dog. Annette placed first in a short story contest even though (or because) Rebel had planted a muddy foot print in the middle of the first page, and she didn't have a chance to retype it. It's one of the favorite family legends, either because Rebel was part of the story or because Annette was both idiosyncratic and talented.

There's also the family story when my father-in-law threw the dining room chairs out in the yard after my toddler son slipped between the seat and the shoulder rest of one of the chairs and fell on his head. My father-in-law bought new chairs the following day—captain's chairs with enough dowel work that not even a snake could slide between those rungs. It doesn't take a rocket scientist to figure out the reason why we retell that story over and over: 1) Grandpa cared for his grandkids. 2) He was wont to use inappropriate gestures to prove it.

Other family legends are told for their magical or unexplained qualities, a facet of family legends that also need to be told. In every family history, there are unexplainable moments, a pivotal time when someone believes in a dream or follows an urge out of nowhere. It's not my place to elaborate on the meaning of these stories although I think that, since they turn up over and over again in family legends, they are meant to send a message that each family is touched by a universal presence that is bigger than themselves.

These stories are important in your memoir collection. Sooner or later they may die out when the older story tellers leave the family circle. Someday there will be grandchildren and great-grandchildren who will want to know those stories in their entirety. That's why it's important to commit them to the written word. At this point, Grandpa's story and daughter Annette's victory story are still in the family's repertoire, but if you are a family of story tellers, every generation adds to the family legend collection, and I have several stories from grandchildren as well.

Write your family legend, including the unexplainable and fantastic, as if you were sitting around a campfire or a kitchen table with your family. Explain the genealogy of the characters as the Bible does: 'My dad's mother that would have been your great-grandmother, her name was Anna and she was married to your great-grandfather Trombley' etc. This may require research; looking through old photos, letters, journals, interviewing other family members, etc. If you can't find the details you want, write the story anyway.

This is a recipe from Mom with a little story that she told, not a 'family' story, but rather a folk tale that she told and we remember every time we eat soup. I'm working on a children's picture book to illustrate the story. Wouldn't you know, in researching, I found this folk tale (minus Mom's recipe) told in three different forms in other parts of the world.

Chicken Noodles

Cut up one chicken and simmer the back, neck and all the parts you don't want to use for fried chicken. Cook celery and onions in a separate pot and add to the chicken broth after you've taken out the bones from the chicken stock.

While the chicken cooks, make noodles with 5 cups of flour, a dash of salt, eight eggs and a bit of oil. Knead and roll out as thin as possible. Cut into strips and drop into boiling chicken stock. Cook for fifteen-twenty minutes.

Once upon a time a poor old lady made chicken soup just as I told you. She was ready to sit down and eat when there was a knock on the door. When she opened the door, a man, weary and dirty from long miles of traveling, stood there. He asked if she had anything at all for him to eat if only a crust of bread. The old lady took pity on him and invited him in and shared her soup with him. When he was finished, he thanked her. He said he didn't know how to repay her, but he took out his change purse and gave her a dollar for each little fat bubble that floated on the soup.

Since the old lady was poor and so were the chickens, the fat globules that floated on her soup were small but many and so the man gave her many dollars.

The old lady, overwhelmed with gratitude at her good fortune, told her neighbor about the good man. The neighbor had seen the nondescript man in the neighborhood and would never have guessed he had so much money to give away. She followed the old lady's recipe, but her chickens were as fat as she was and to be sure her broth would be even better than her neighbor's, she added an extra scoop of chicken fat from the last chicken she had cooked.

Sure enough, the beggar arrived at her door and asked if she had anything for him to eat and she proudly served him her chicken soup. When he finished, he thanked her for her hospitality and said that he would pay her for each fat bubble that floated on the soup. Unfortunately, the soup was so laden with chicken fat that the whole surface was one big bubble and the greedy lady received one dollar.

In Mom's story the traveler was Jesus.

This story, also one of Mom's, I originally published in "Sunshine Magazine". It's one of those unexplainable times that happen in a family and told over and over until it has become one of the family legends.

Mom's Prayer

My mother tells of the time when my brother came home from the army. He was twenty-one then and full of post-war depression. He drank heavily and seemed blind to the part of life that wasn't sad or brutal. The letter that told her he was coming home filled her with motherly anticipation and she cleaned and aired the house and made ready his bed. Since my sister Lillian had been killed in a car accident less than a year before, Mom put even more heart into her vigil than usual.

One night before Elmer's anticipated arrival, she awoke in the darkness, wishing once again she could dream of Lillian so she could see her and hear her again. Then a voice said so clear she almost thought someone had spoken aloud, "Lillian is okay, pray for Elmer." She pushed her way out of the bed-covers and had a strong feeling someone was in the house. She went to Elmer's bedroom, but it was untouched. She went downstairs into the kitchen and snapped on the light. Something made her walk to the calendar and point to the date and then trace slowly the days until Elmer would be home. She dropped to her knees by the kitchen table and prayed like only a mother can pray for one of her own.

Elmer came home a day later than his scheduled day and Mom told him about her overpowering need to pray for him.

Elmer in turn confessed the reason for his late arrival. He had been sitting at a bar in California celebrating his return from post-war Japan. Fortunately, he had sewn much of his severance pay into an inner pocket. As the crowd thinned, two men who had been watching him as he drank, attacked him when he left, beat him and rolled him into an alley. After taking the little money he had left in his wallet, they left him bleeding and unconscious.

A man found him much later. He looked at the discarded wallet and found Elmer's papers. He took him to a hotel and asked the clerk to take care of him. When Elmer revived and found that he had not only been saved but that his hotel bill had been paid by the stranger, he asked the manager for the man's name so that he could thank and repay him. The manager told him that the man had put the room in Elmer's name, but he said that Elmer's rescuer walked the bars where the returning soldiers stopped to see if anyone needed help. His own son was in the service and he hoped someone would help his boy if he needed it.

When Mom heard his story, she asked Elmer what night it was that the stranger rescued him. Elmer went to the calendar and pointed to the very night that Mom had traced with her fingers before she knelt by the kitchen table to pray. Mom told us that story several times to boost faith in the goodness of others and a power greater than our own.

Recipe Exercises

- Use a family recipe to write your memory of the person, place or time you received it. This may be as short as a couple of paragraphs or could be an extended character description or a complete scene.

- Create a scene around a family meal time. Include setting, dialogue and description of food served.

- Make a list of favorite family foods. Who likes fish, steak, pasta? Who is a vegetarian? A vegan? Write a philosophy of your family based on their food preferences.

- Make up a goofy recipe of your family such as: Put one father (description) together with one son/daughter (description), stir vigorously, bake on a hot summer day or chill on a January night, describe the concoction.

- Invent a goofy recipe that includes ingredients of favorite recipes collected over the years: Mix one trout with rigatoni and stir vigorously, etc.

- Invent a recipe of family or friends that reflects your reality: Take one good barbeque day, add one son with a mission to grill enough hamburgers to feed an army, etc.

- Construct a recipe for a.) a perfect day, b.) a perfect job, c.) a perfect shopping trip, d.) a family holiday, etc.

Family Legend Exercises

- Make a list of family stories that have been told several times.

- Find the reason (the 'moral' of the story) for each of these stories.

- Write one of these stories. Add details that are never included in the spoken version.

- Repeat number three with several of your family legends.If your story is about an individual's strength, perseverance, patience etc., write a character sketch of the individual. Include details of appearance, mannerisms, etc.

- Examine a family legend and see if and how it fits into the bigger legends. Do you have a prodigal son story in your family? A Red Riding Hood tale? Can you write or rewrite your family story with comparisons to these universal legends?

- Play a game with your family. Who are you as a fairy tale character or a mythical hero? Example: I am one of the three little pigs because ___" Or try this with a family member labeling another. Example: "I think you are one of the three little pigs because"____. Keep it funny and light.

Section Eleven

Collage

Writers are scavengers, always scrounging
for language and images to illuminate their work.

– Lou Willett Stanek

Writers truly are scavengers for "images to illuminate their work" and Stanek's quote probably captures the writer's spirit of collage much better that Webster's New World Dictionary's definition: "An art form in which bits of objects, as newspaper, cloth, leaves, etc. are pasted together on a surface or a composition so made".

The visual form was elevated to the notice of the art establishment by Picasso and his contemporaries but, in reading about decorative homemade art, 'ordinary' women used collage to arrange and display important mementos years before Picasso—the graduation picture with tassel and boutonniere attached, the wedding memorabilia with a photo, a napkin or a snippet of flower. Collage is neither linear nor chronological. Rather, it is an imagistic impression of a character or event. Nothing is ordered chronologically, yet the arrangement expresses the whole.

Scrapbooking has taken the creative arts into a whole industry of tools, patterned and/or textured papers, and books of advice on how to master this latest impulse to collage form. I'm a passionate scrapbooker myself since I've accumulated so many memory scraps, but creating a collage demands careful planning before you cut and snip irreplaceable mementos: The lace or ribbon from your wedding bouquet may be too long, the brochure you brought back from that last trip too cumbersome, and the photo that you love has unnecessary background. On the other hand, a collage of cherished items can be so much more effective and accessible in an artful arrangement than hidden in a cedar chest. If you scrapbook, you already know that color, design and layout make an appealing page. In putting together memorabilia, give yourself entirely to a character or a time. Each piece is part of your impression of the memory and each adds texture to the whole picture.

The last visual collage I did was a 'Mom' photo collage. It took me a week fumbling and organizing before I got up the courage to pick up the scissors and cut and paste twelve photos. As I arranged and rearranged those pictures, several possibilities came to mind. Some of the pictures were the face of a woman in her forties. Some were the image of a strong woman in her seventies. Was the collage about the evolution of a woman from young mother to wise crone? Some photos were with children, some with a flower, some with a book. Was the collage about the grand sweep of lifetime interests compressed into a single visual? I gained enough inspiration from putting together one collage to write more than one story of the mother I remember.

Photos are an obvious collage material, but collage, as Webster says, uses other materials as well. One of my friends sent her sister a playful card with seashells, sand, and bits of dried ocean grass as well as a photo of her on a Florida beach. The textures, as well as the arrangement, were a wonderful visual statement about her Florida experience, and the visual statement led her to create a poem to accompany her visual collage.

Although collage seems to border more on a discussion of the visual arts, it has possibilities for memoir. A scrapbook of those treasured memory scraps artfully arranged can also include poetry, character sketches, letters and recipes—a potpourri of memories that mix several forms.

Words and phrases can also work as a collage in themselves, each word adding to the memory you attempt to evoke. The example at the end of this section is a word collage taken from my mother's journals. I have a whole box of Mom's journals, and even though they are the written words of my deceased parent, reading each page of those day-by-day entries is something my children or grandchildren may never do. I wanted to preserve Mom's words in a more accessible form by extracting the essence of those pages and omitting repetitive reports on weather and the state of the peonies (Most habitual journalers tend to repeat), but certain words and phrases 'stuck out'. They appeared and reappeared, phrased differently.

Omitting repetition brings the character's concerns into clear focus, which is the advantage of a word collage. The imagistic impression of a character or event is what you are attempting, but it is important that you choose the lines that convey that image in the clearest way possible. If I had cut and pasted without thought, my mother might have looked like someone obsessed with weather or peonies.

I highlighted those words and phrases and then cut them out. I didn't actually cut up the journal pages. I copied the highlighted parts, put them on my table, and shoved them around until they came together. Meaningful arrangement is the fun and challenge with collage, whether it's photos, objects or words. It's obvious that I used the same technique with my word collage that Chris Lucka used in condensing and arranging her aunt's words from several letters to create her found poetry. Since I hesitate to think of my efforts as poetry, I offer the example as a word collage in the way I cut, pasted and arranged words and phrases to create a meaningful memory and a theme of Mom's concerns in her last years.

Is this honest? Is this the way to go through another's prose and reconstruct it? I certainly would never attempt this with someone's published work and present it as their prose in toto, and I cannot say for certain that my word collage is what Mom's journal theme was about, no more that I can interpret Picasso's collages as his exact intent. It is often easier to find the words and phrases in other's words to express who they are, or at least your perception of who they are. When you try this technique with your own journals in the most honest way possible, certain themes will emerge in your own life and make collage a valuable one in self-discovery. With my photo collages, with my word collages from Mom's journals, I interpreted who Mom was from my perception. And I believe, whether it be a Picasso or my mother's journals, that is what memoir is about.

Theme

In working with collage, whether scrapbooking or finding words and phrases in a journal or a letter, a central idea emerges that brings together those accumulated bits of information. Often the central idea comes as a surprise. My own memoir began as a scrapbook that used several of the prompts I've described in the past sections with not much organization. I confess that I never saw family as the theme of my own memoir until I put it in order to use examples for this book. As I said earlier, it's often easier to see in other's words who they are or your perception of who they are, so my belated revelation may come as no surprise to my readers.

This section differs from the other sections in this book since there are no simple techniques to construct theme, but rather to analyze what you have already written. If you've looked at various books on writing, you may have noticed that discussion never begins with theme. It starts with a character, a place, a time and the theme emerges after the words are written. McCauley and Lanning say,

> "Real life may have no ready-made plots, but it does have recurring patterns and forms. We are born, we mature, we grow old, and we die. But, within that given form for human lives, there is a more specific cycle that most of us share... There is no mystery as to why most people have always preferred a story with a beginning, middle, and an end. The pattern is copied from the human tale itself."

In tracing a story with that specific cycle, life stories delineate a theme without conscious planning and unfolds in a way that follows a central thread of truth for the character, which in this case is very important, because the character is you. Grounding your world, characterizing the people who inhabit that world, and the emotional and the factual elements of your life all contribute to the overall message that your stories have. We can elaborate or embroider dialogue, we can even be vague about the exact chronology of our stories, as in the preceding section on family legends, but stories should never begin with theme in mind such as a vendetta, excuses for what we've done or not done, or a parade of our virtues or vices. Life's themes arise from the drama of real life and come from the inside of life in all its shame and glory, love and hate—human dramas that bring us to realize—or to wonder.

The cause and effect of life's choices give us our life's possibilities or dead-ends and raises questions: 'if I had married Len instead of Larry', 'if I had taken that job', 'if I hadn't been so timid'; if... if... if... Why did I make that choice? What did I plan to effect? These considerations may give you hours of thought as you ponder the emergent theme of the stories you have written. You will find a thread that runs through your life as surely as if you had planned it, although at the time you fell in love, or took that first job, you may have had no idea what that design would be.

Theme answers 'What is the story about?' in one defining sentence. 'The story is about coming of age in the early 1900's'. Asking and clearly answering that question will give you the title for the work and will bring about revision so each sentence, each paragraph illustrates, describes, uses appropriate metaphors, and points back to the title, the organizing idea.. Coming into womanhood through the details of my mother's experiences as a rural farm girl will be a much different memoir than my granddaughter's story even if the theme is the same. In either case, neither Mom nor my granddaughter scribbled poems or impressions in a journal with 'coming into womanhood' as a conscious theme.

In answering the question, "What is the story about?" a theme examines characters, possibilities, raises questions, and imagines consequences of action. The cause-and-effect that fiction writers build into a story attempts to mimic real life choices. Chance or coincidence in life is often neither, but more like a stream that comes to a shoal and diverges to create a new stream bed. Within the master plot of each life—birth to death—are those shoals, those obstacles that create the scenes that fill in the individual plot of a life.

Even as 'What is the story about?' is an important question to ask, a related question arises: 'Why did I write this story?" the question posed in the introduction. At that time, that question was posed to focus on the possible audience; yourself (self-discovery), family, or the world at large. However, after putting together the words you have written and finding a theme, the answer to that question may have changed. The journal entries, the poetry, the character sketches you simply meant to find your own grounding may have turned out to be something that the whole family needs to know. Or the family stories you constructed has a strong universal theme that should be published for a wider audience. As Burroway says,

> "Literature is stuck with ideas in a way other arts are not. Music, paradoxically the most abstract of the arts, creates a logical structure that need make no reference to the world outside itself. It may express a mood, but it need draw no conclusions. Shapes in painting and sculpture may suggest forms in the physical world, but they need not represent the world, and they need not contain a message. But words mean."

"Words mean". What a wonderful and powerful fact! By the way words come together, we express the 'what' and 'why' of life. And the what and why are the elements that construct theme. When you put yourself in the story and let the words tell the reader what you see and hear as honestly as you can, the theme, the 'why' will not need to be written out as the 'moral' as in Aesop's fables. It will emerge in the 'what' of your story.

The words are exact quotations lifted from three consecutive pages of Mom's writing. I see Mom on her porch as clearly as if I had read pages of her journals.

From Mom's Journals

This is Sunday—went to Mass.
We've been having a lot of rain.
Maybe I'll have to unload the stuff in the bedroom
Tomorrow.
Monday—got up early
Having my coffee on the porch at 8:15.

I thought I saw Nancy going to mail a letter
wearing her white sweater.
Around 11:00 a.m.—
It turned cloudy.
I don't see Tom around.
The pink peonies are still in bloom.
The one by the barn has ten blooms.
I cut three for my bouquet—
The bush had thirteen flowers.
I am still thinking about the rosebud
that I left behind in Grand Rapids.
That head of mine just makes me forget things.
I'm sorry.

Before you pick up scissors and cut and paste, remember the person on the other side of the pen. The pieces saved and arranged are taken out of a more complete context of another's words. It is important to preserve the essence of the writer's character with honesty and respect.

Collage Exercises

- ☙ Imagine yourself as a child living in the home you now occupy. Write what you see, hear, feel. Use words or phrases from your writing to construct a word collage.

- ☙ Imagine your son/daughter living in the home of your childhood. Write what she/he might see, hear, and feel. Do the same as in exercise one.

- ☙ Clip pictures, words, etc. from magazines that appeal to you. Don't think. Just clip a pile. Arrange and glue them on a background in a way that you feel expresses who you are. You might use this as an illustration for a section of your memoir.

- ☙ Choose two random photos in your collection (Close your eyes and randomly point to make your picks). Write, linking the two.

- Choose words and phrases from several pages of your journal. Copy them on separate slips of paper as I outlined with Mom's journals. It's important that you separate and play at rearranging.

- Try mixing bits of recipes, letters, family legends etc. in a kaleidoscope of words and phrases. Add a few photos or drawings and decorate a page of your memoir with the collage.

Theme Exercises

- Look through the memoir pieces you have written so far. Is there a certain idea, philosophy, mode of acting that reappears repeatedly? Write a description of your observations.

- Practice finding theme in books or films that you know. Write them out in one sentence.

- Try reconstructing the outcome of a story in a favorite book or film by finding where the main character's choices affected the outcome. What in the character's personality caused him/her to make those choices?

- List themes you have noticed in films or books.

- Try exercise two with your own life stories.

Section Twelve

Putting It Together

On the continuum of time between past and future,
the present moment is the point of power from which you can
influence the meaning and direction of your life.

– Tristine Rainier

In the first section, I compared writing a memoir to pieces of a jig-saw puzzle; the pieces fashioned from photos, treasured objects, family recipes, etc. Now that you have gone through all these sections or some of these sections, you will have noticed what appealed to you and what did not appeal to you at all. And I didn't even address travel as a possible memoir organizer. A pen friend who travels and keeps extensive notes wrote her memoir as a travel journal, filling in her travel experiences with her personal life. When she was in India and looking at Hinduism, she compared that religious philosophy with her own. When she was in Japan, she compared life style and family mores. It is a memoir that not many of us can produce.

In like manner, your memoir will be built around who you are and how you express yourself, whether photos or family recipes or music inspires your stories. Perhaps you're an eclectic and will do your memoirs in the spirit of this book—some photos, some family recipes, some found poetry, a 'scrapbook' approach. In all sections to this point, we have talked about family stories as pattern pieces with no concern of chronological order.

I purposefully avoided autobiography, organized by time, that too often can fall into a predictable pattern that many write with the sound of 'last dying breath' instead of living vitality. Nevertheless, good autobiographies fill bookshelves with lively stories, personal philosophy and settings and characters that rival any good work of fiction. Now that you have accessed several stories and dodged an outline that implies plodding through time markers, perhaps an autobiography is the form that fits your words.

Most of the writing techniques already discussed apply to autobiographical form, but "What is this story about?" and "Why now?" are especially important. Celebrities write autobiographies (or have them ghost-written) because the public wants to know how and why they're celebrities. The rest of us rely on a strong message of survival, adventure or personal wisdom to capture the reader. Abilities, interests and achievements carry an autobiography. If you are interested in insects, you acquire a microscope, your science experiment in high school earns a blue ribbon at the science fair, and you take a trip down the Amazon and collect rare specimens, the autobiography has a clear focus. Throw out stories of your first day in kindergarten unless it relates to an ability, an interest or an achievement. On the other hand, keep stories that illustrate the interest or the ability that has gone wrong. Your interest in insects hatched a swarm of renegade fruit flies that embarrassed Mother hosting a book club when she offered guests a plate of pineapple and watermelon.

An autobiography or a fully-narrated memoir may have its own time markers that ground a reader, but if your memoir is as loose as a scrapbook, it will need some kind of timeline. I like the look, the feel of a horizontal time line: Birth down to the present, years marked off on a neat black line that cuts through two facing 8 x 11 pages. But usually there is not enough room on that neat black line to record a personal history that has added text. A vertical system works well: 1942: I was born on February 10th. The Second World War was in full swing—A time line can be an independent appendage to your stories, a reference at the front or back of your collection, a piece of historical data to which your readers can refer to for time orientation. In section five, time was an important part of setting, but time was part of an organic piece with the right details for your personal story. You don't have to make it painfully and artificially clear about world events that subtly influenced the story.

A time line can free you instead of becoming this constrictive device that insists on your stories coming out in a predictable order, which is why a time line is in this final section. We *are* part of a bigger world picture but often we don't realize it until much later. My life story would have been different if the 'small farm' wasn't exterminated when I was around thirteen. Yet, at thirteen, I had no idea that I was experiencing my first brush with political-economic America. If I had constructed a timeline first, stories of those years would be influenced by those realizations and lose that feeling of "the present moment {as} the point of power" that Tristine Rainier says can be the direction of a life. When the story happens at thirteen or thirty, it can only be from that "present moment of power".

It's the wonderful and mysterious way each life is worked out, a single thread on an immense tapestry. We don't know how our lives fill that tapestry's design no more than a thread in a Persian carpet realizes its part of the whole. But it's the reason to research and record the bigger context around your life. You will discover, in building a time line, how your life was affected by the world around you; or you will not realize it but the reader of your stories will. Either way, the research will be a valuable addition to your collection of stories.

Timeline Exercises

- ∾ Use photos with extended captions to fix time and place. Use an organizing line on which to hang your photos (The line will again be vertical).

- ∾ If you are artistic, decorate your time line with drawings.

- ∾ Color code your time line. Red: passionate points. Blue, sad. Etc. Or, on a more conventional note, color code the personal data versus the historical information. With today's color printers, this would not be difficult. Or use paint or markers (I still like the messy and time- consuming hands-on way of doing things.)

- ∾ Revisit that checker board idea in section one's exercises. Draw a chess board (you in the middle) and arrange the events of your life in order of importance around your central point on the board.

∞ Is there a way you can make your time line look like the Freitag Pyramid? (Rising scenes, major epiphanies in your life?) Who said a time line had to be *flat*?

∞ Possible time line marks:

> Birth
> First school
> Moves
> Graduations
> Birthdays (exceptional ones)
> Catastrophes (accidents, injuries, prolonged illnesses)
> Deaths, births, and marriages that affected you
> First job (other jobs?)
> Your own marriage or love affairs
> Children and/or grandchildren

Specials: Medals of service, promotions, certificates of recommendation, etc.

Personal specials: First time white water rafting, first time you won in Las Vegas, etc.

Possible Forms Your Memoir Might Take

∞ An ABC book that uses the alphabet to introduce major people, places, things or concepts of your life. A is for art or A is for daughter Ann followed by a short story. B is for bat or Bill, etc. The collection could be illustrated with photos, line drawings, cartoons or a combination.

∞ A book of your own poetry or prose poetry (this could also be illustrated).

- A photo collection with accompanying character sketches or fully drawn stories.

- A recipe book that includes family sayings, descriptions of the family kitchen, family legends, scenes around the family meals, etc.

- A collection of letters that you write to family and/or friends about people and places you have known. The collection could also include letters received in their entirety or in a found poetry collage.

- A book of cartoons about family and neighborhood events.

- A book of annotated lists, with items on each list written about more extensively.

Or a combination book that uses several of these ideas in a scrap-book form.

Ways to Put Your Life Stories Together

- Use photos. Scan pictures into your story collection. Or use a photo to introduce each section. Construct a photo album that uses extended captions to describe the people and places in your life.

- Use your artistic talent. Accompany stories with line drawings. Illustrate the cover of your collection with your own art. Draw cartoon strips of humorous life episodes.

- Create a collage. Use photos, swatches of material, magazine pictures that say something about you. Use as a cover for your collection or as a frontispiece.

- Use family recipes, either as incidental pieces in your collection or as the organizing theme where each recipe would preface a family story. Invent recipes, humorous or instructive: "Recipe for Getting Through a Weekend with Four Teenage Kids" or "My Recipe for Being a Parent".

∽ Cue your stories around the music you love. Make CDs of the music and keep in an envelope glued to the story collection.

∽ Preface your stories with poetry—your own or a poem you love. Use poetic devices in your collection, such as alliterative titles (My Medieval Mother) or titling each section with a metaphor (My Mother The Volcano). Intersperse your stories with short poems or metaphors that say something important about you.

∽ Use important objects in your life to center your stories. Take a picture or draw each object to preface the stories.

∽ Use several of these ideas together to create a collection that is a montage of recipes, photos, drawings, music, etc.

Final Thoughts

Good stories are not written as much as *rewritten*—and written again. It is important that you have a good grasp of technique so that your editing will yield the best work possible. Revisit section two often. As you continue to write, critique will inform the revision of your work. Writing is an ever-evolving process, and every new story brings new challenges and new discoveries, the wonderful frustration and the fascination with the dance of words. After all is said and done, I know of no shortcut, no "Six Easy Steps to Writing Like a Pro". Writing just gets better by writing and reading the work of the masters.

Constant writing is obvious, but I cannot emphasize enough the role that critical reading plays in a writer's development. The writers you love are your coaches. They show how it's done. Writers read in a different way. One of my friends said that she should never have started writing because she can't read a trashy novel anymore without thinking how it could be better or different. I'm sorry this book didn't include critical reading of the masters, but that would take another book. Look at the problems you have in your own writing (every writer has them), read and reread your favorite authors and see how they handle that problem. Are you weak on characterization? What does your author do? Find paragraphs, sentences, or words and underline them. How does your author get that characterization in there? Dialogue? Action? Thought? I hope the bibliography will be a part of your team of coaches, but I also hope that the suggestions will be a spur for you to build a roster of your own.

Just as a story's end often comes around and repeats the beginning, this is a revisiting of the writing process. For me, jumping off into writing that first draft has always been the most difficult part of writing. The demons of doubt fill my space and mutter 'you can't', 'this is dumb', and 'this isn't worth writing'. I'm constantly on the lookout for ways to trick the demons until I have produced that ball of clay. I hope this book has helped you trick the demons and that your writing process is pulling ever more and better stories from your life on to the page.

I couldn't stand to be here if I didn't make a stain upon the silence.

– Samuel Beckett

Acknowledgements

No writer writes alone. I owe a debt of gratitude to Chris Lucka, an editor with an iron hand in a velvet glove, MidMichigan Writers who demonstrated over and over again the value of critique, and the members of my memoir classes who taught me that life stories are the best stories of all.

Glossary

Adjective: A word used to qualify or limit a noun. Example: Two horses limits the noun 'horse'. Purple sky qualifies the noun 'sky'.

Adverb: A word used to describe a verb, an adjective or another adverb. Examples: Derek was warmly introduced (warmly describes the verb introduced), the audience loudly, cheerily welcomed Derek (loudly describes another adverb 'cheerily'), Derek's ruddily red face turned purple (ruddily describes the adjective red). Adverbs should be used sparingly!

Analogy: A comparison of one thing to another by certain points such as function. Example: Derek runs as fast as a deer. Derek's speed is the point of function compared.

Autobiography: Story of one's own life written or dictated by oneself.

Biography: Story of a life written by another.

Characterization: Description of a person by specific details such as apparel, speech, mannerisms, etc.

Character sketch: A brief description of a person, with details as above, but used as a stand-alone piece, whereas characterization is more often a term for a character in a larger work.

Cliché: An expression or idea over used. Examples: green as grass, black as night.

Climax: The highest point of interest, drama, or excitement in a story when the tension of the story is addressed and resolved.

Collage: An art form in which bits of objects are pieced together in no chronological order. Word collages may form found poetry or an imagistic impression taken from a longer piece of narrative.

Comparison: To examine for likenesses or differences. Example: Her hair was like spaghetti. Often, comparisons are limited to two objects or ideas that are opposite (gold vs. lead, justice vs. slavery), but comparisons can also compare qualities shared with subtle differences (Both women's hair shone—Dianne's with a blond radiance and Debra's with a dark sheen).

Contrast: A striking difference in two things compared.

Critique: An analysis or evaluation. Since the French derivative of the word is so close to 'critic' and therefore 'criticize', it often has a negative connotation, but effective critique (analysis) is a writer's best friend.

Dialogue: Conversation between two or more people, usually indicated by quotation marks. A paragraph change signals the reader to a change in speaker.

Dissonance: A discord or lack of harmony. Stories always have this element that creates tension between what the character wants and what obstacles stand in his/her way.

Essay: A personal literary composition to analyze or interpret. Essays can range from analyzing the way a frog swims to interpreting the meaning of Ghandi's words of advice.

Freitag's Pyramid: A diagram of story form that plots scenes of rising tension to a climactic scene that resolves the story problem and falls into an ending scene or narrative.

Flash fiction: A very short story (500 words or less). Memoir writers can adapt this form for nonfiction also. In spite of its brevity, flash fiction poses a story problem, action, and solution.

Legend: A story handed down for generations in a certain group of people and popularly believed to have a historical basis.

Memoir: A record of events based on the writer's personal observations.

Metaphor: To speak of one thing as if was another. Example: Lillian was a flower, scented and frilly, and always bending toward the sun.

Myth: A traditional story to explain nature, the origin of man, or the customs and religious rites of a people. A mythology is a collection of these stories, such as a Greek or Native American mythology.

Narrative: The way a story is related and carries the voice or tone of the writer (or narrator).

Noun: Words that name a person, place, thing, or idea. Boy and truth are both nouns. Concrete nouns, such as boy, are those that can be detected through the senses. Abstract nouns, such as truth, are ideas and more difficult for a reader to visualize.

Passive verb/voice: Is, are, was, were, am, seem are passive verbs or verbs of 'being' as opposed to verbs of action, such as run, jump, etc. A narrative that uses too many passive verbs lapses into a passive voice. Keep passive verbs to a minimum.

Perception shift: When a story's hero/ine becomes aware of a difference in reality as s/he had perceived it. Example: Donna realizes her son is not her little boy but a grown man. A well-plotted story usually involves a perception shift in the main character.

Plot: The plan of action in a story. The plot usually involves a number of scenes and can be diagrammed as a Freitag Pyramid of rising tension to resolution of a story problem.

Point of view: The choice of narrator's perspective in a story. First person ('I'), second person ('you'), third person ('s/he'). Point of view choice affects the distance between writer and reader.

Preposition: A word of relation, such as in, by, with, below, etc. (anywhere you could put yourself in relation to a box). A prepositional phrase consists of the preposition and its object, such as 'into the box', 'by the box', etc. Prepositional phrases can slow a sentence and two or more together should be avoided. Do not end a sentence with a preposition.

Prewrite: Step one of the writing process, finding the idea. All writers prewrite by taking notes, journaling, or interior monologue. The prompts included in this book are meant to elicit the prewrite phase.

Prose: The ordinary form of language without rhyme or meter.

Prose Poem: A short piece of writing in the ordinary language form, but incorporates poetic devices, such as metaphor, simile, etc.

Simile: A figure of speech in which one thing is compared to another. Example: Ben was like a jack-in-the-box.

Style: Characteristic manner of expression. A writer's style may be humorous, sarcastic, earnest, and is characterized by selection of details, choice of describing words, etc.

Symbol: An object used to represent something abstract, such as a dove symbolizes peace, the cross represents Christianity, etc.

Theme: A unifying idea expressed throughout a work with related variations.

Tone: A way of wording or expressing things that displays a certain attitude. Tone and style are similar.

Transition: A word, phrase or sentence that signals a change from one scene to another.

Verb: A word that denotes action or state of being. Verbs may be expressed as present (I run), past (I ran), or past perfect (I have or had run). Narrative should stay in the same verb tense.

Voice: The means by which something is expressed, similar to style and tone.

Works Cited

Albert, Susan Wittig. *Writing From Life*. New York: Tarcher/Putnam, 1996.

Browne, Renni, Dave King. *Self-Editing For Fiction Writers*. New York: HarperCollins, 1993.

Burroway, Janet. *Writing Fiction, A Guide to Narrative Craft*. New York: HarperCollins, 1996.

Cate, Curtis. George Sand. New York: Avon Books, 1975.

Conroy, Pat. *My Reading Life*. Random House, 2010.

DeMarchi, Tom. "Dancing About Architecture: Popular Music and Writing". *The Writer's Chronicle 33.4* (2001): 22-29.

Edwards, Betty. *Drawing on the Right Side of the Brain*. Los Angeles: J.P. Tarcher, 1979.

Holroyd, Michael. "In Search of Narrative Truth". *Poets and Writers Jan/Feb 2001*: 14-18.

McGregor, Michael. "An Interview with Kent Haruf". *The Writer's Chronicle 33.5* (2001): 38-45.

Nicolaides, Kimon. *The Natural Way to Draw*. Boston: Houghton Mifflin, 1969.

Rainier, Tristine. *The New Diary*. Los Angeles: J.P. Tarcher, 1978.

Rico, Gabriele Lusser. *Writing the Natural Way*. Los Angeles: J.P. Tarcher, 1983.

Stanek, Lou Willett. *Writing Your Life*. New York: Avon Books, 1996.

Steinberg, Michael. "Editor's Notes." Editorial. *Fourth Genre 1.1* (1999): v-viii.

Welty, Eudora. *One Writer's Beginnings*. Massachusetts: Harvard Univ. Press, 1984.

Annotated Reading List

Barrington, Judith. **Writing the Memoir**. Eighth Mountain Press, 1997. *A practical guide to the personal challenges and ethical dilemmas in writing true stories.*

Bragg, Rick. **All Over but the Shoutin'**. Vintage Books, 1997. *A gritty memoir of growing up dirt poor in the South. Against all odds, Bragg becomes a Pulitzer Prize winner as a reporter for the New York Times.*

Bullfinch's Mythology. New York: Doubleday, 1968. *A nineteenth-century Boston banker, Thomas Bullfinch, originally gathered together Greek myths referred to in literature and poetry and his work is still considered a standard reference for Greek myths.*

Campbell, Joseph. **Hero with a Thousand Masks**. Pantheon, 1949. Reprinted Princeton University Press, 2004. *Campbell's theory of human connectedness with countless examples of similar ancient myths and folktales is one of several of his thought-provoking works.*

Christensen, Kate. **Blue Plate Special: An Autobiography of My Appetites**. Doubleday, 2013. *Christensen records and describes meals that mark a fifty-year life journey of loss and discovery.*

Dillard, Annie. **The Writing Life**. Harper Perennial, 1989. *Advice and encouragement for a writer fills this slim volume.*

Holley, Tara Elgin with Joe Holley. **My Mother's Keeper**. William Morrow and Co., 1997. *A daughter's memoir of growing up in the shadow of her mother's schizophrenia.*

Karr, Mary. **The Liars' Club**. Penguin House, 1995. *Karr's first memoir of her childhood in a gritty southeast Texas town is told with a naïve honesty and humor.*

Kirkland, Gelsey with Greg Lawrence. **Dancing on My Grave**. Doubleday, 1986. *Kirkland's autobiography of the trials and triumphs of a ballet dancer at the New York City Ballet.*

Lamott, Anne. **Bird by Bird**. Pantheon Books, 1994. *Whatever you write, Lamott's book on the way of the writer combines instruction with wry inspiration.*

McCourt, Frank. **Angela's Ashes**.

Nafisi, Azar. **Reading Lolita in Tehran**. Random House, 2003. *A fascinating glimpse into the world of young, educated woman in 21st century Iran.*

Reichl, Ruth. **Tender at the Bone: Growing up at the Table**. Random House, 1998. *Reichl's memoir of growing up with dysfunction is told with wry humor*

Stillman, Peter. **Families Writing**. Writers Digest Books, 1989. *Packed with ideas for families to write together.*

The Norton Book of Personal Essays. Edited by Joseph Epstein. W.W. Norton & Co., 1997. *This is a wonderful resource for anyone interested in writing personal essay. Voices from Mark Twain to Amy Tan are a great read.*

Wall, Jeanette. **The Glass Castle**. Scribner, 2006. *Walls' memoir opens with a scene that reflects her rootless and often homeless life growing up so powerfully, the reader HAS to read on.*

White, E.B. **Once More to the Lake**, Essays by E.B. White. Harper &Row, 1977, 197-202. *E.B. White's essays are great examples of a master of the essay form, and "Once More to the Lake" is the brightest star in his repertoire.*

www.ingramcontent.com/pod-product-compliance
Lightning Source LLC
Chambersburg PA
CBHW060758050426
42449CB00008B/1443